Dead Men Walking
Volume Two
50 American Killers Who
Were Executed for Their Crimes

Robert Keller

Please Leave Your Review of This Book At
http://bit.ly/kellerbooks

ISBN-13: 978-1720679097
ISBN-10: 1720679096

© 2018 by Robert Keller

robertkellerauthor.com

All rights reserved.

No part of this publication may be copied or reproduced in any format, electronic or otherwise, without the prior, written consent of the copyright holder and publisher. This book is for informational and entertainment purposes only and the author and publisher will not be held responsible for the misuse of information contain herein, whether deliberate or incidental.

Much research, from a variety of sources, has gone into the compilation of this material. To the best knowledge of the author and publisher, the material contained herein is factually correct. Neither the publisher, nor author will be held responsible for any inaccuracies.

Table of Contents

Lynda Block & George Sibley Jr. 7

Mark Stroman 11

Robert Carter 15

George Hassell 19

John Taylor 23

Wanda Jean Allen 27

Earl Frederick 31

David Alan Gore 35

Lonnie Johnson 39

Cameron Willingham 43

Sterling Rault 47

Hans Schmidt 51

Thomas J. Grasso 55

Newton Anderson 59

Bennie Demps 63

Charles Anthony Boyd 67

Carl Eugene Kelly 71

William Woratzeck 75

Jason Getsy 79

Arthur Waite 83

Mark Hopkinson 87

Will Lockett	91
Rocky Barton	95
Alton Coleman	99
Daryl Mack	103
Thomas Stevens & Christopher Burger	107
Barbara Graham	111
Johnny Ray Johnson	115
Stephen Morin	119
William Wesley Chappell	123
William Hance	127
Elmo Lee Smith	131
Reginald Perkins	135
Dalton Prejean	139
Ellis Wayne Felker	143
Carl Hall & Bonnie Heady	147
Leo Edwards Jr.	151
Kevin Conner	155
Larry Gene Bell	159
Glen McGinnis	163
Buddy Earl Justus	167
William Hickman	171
Steve Roach	175
Charles Brooks Jr.	179
Donald 'Pee Wee' Gaskins	183
Toronto Patterson	187
Christopher Emmett	191

Earle Nelson 195
John Rook 199
Kenneth Biros 203

Lynda Block & George Sibley Jr.

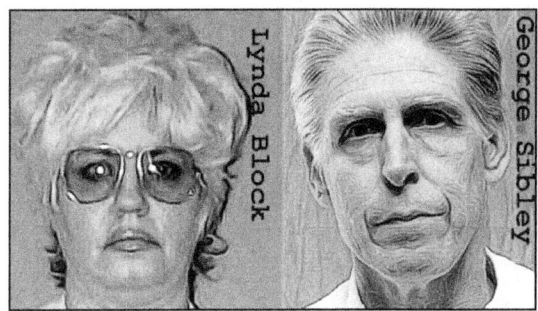

Police Sergeant Roger Motley had only stopped off at the Wal-Mart in Opelika, Alabama, to pick up some supplies for the local jailhouse. But he'd barely entered the store when he was approached by a worried-looking woman. She said that there was a small boy sitting in a car in the parking lot who looked like he may need help. Would the officer check it out? Motley said that he would.

After cruising up and down the rows of parked vehicles for several minutes, Motley eventually came across the car the woman had described, a blue Mustang. Pulling in behind, Motley got out of his patrol car and approached. There was the boy the woman had spoken of, sitting in the back seat. Motley judged him to be nine or ten years old. Behind the wheel sat a gaunt-faced man, probably in his late 40s to early 50s. Tapping on the window, Motley asked the man for his driver's license. The man's response surprised him. He said that he didn't need one. The officer then placed his hand on the butt of his service revolver and ordered the man out of the car. Instead, the man produced a pistol and started shooting.

Motley dived for cover, returning fire as he did so. Then followed an exchange of gunfire that had people screaming and diving for cover as the bullets flew. So concentrated was the officer on the threat in front of him that he failed to notice someone creeping up behind, a blonde-haired woman holding a 9mm Glock pistol. She was right behind him before Motley perceived the threat and turned. By then it was too late. The woman lifted the gun and fired, hitting Motley in the chest. Mortally wounded, the officer staggered toward his patrol car as the woman kept firing. He reached into the vehicle and grabbed the radio handset. "Double zero," was all he managed to say before he collapsed to the ground. (Double zero is the code for "officer needs assistance").

By the time help arrived, the man and woman in the Mustang were long gone. Officer Motley was rushed to the hospital but died that same afternoon. Now a concerted hunt was underway to catch the cop killers, and it soon delivered results. Later that evening, the Mustang was trapped in a police roadblock in Lee County. The killer couple were not about to give up without a fight, though. After releasing the boy, they managed to hold the police at bay for four hours before they eventually ran out of ammunition and were forced to surrender.

George Sibley Jr. and his common-law wife, Lynda Block, were arrested and charged with murder. And it soon emerged why the pair had fought so fiercely to avoid capture. They were fugitives from justice, wanted in Florida for running out on an assault warrant. They were also members of the "Libertarian Party," an anti-establishment movement who believe that the U.S. government has been captured by corrupt bureaucracies and therefore lacks the moral authority to pass laws and collect taxes. "Libertarians" like Block and Sibley therefore declare that they have seceded from the United States and revoke official documents such as birth certificates and passports. This was undoubtedly what Sibley meant when he told officer Motley that he did not need a driver's license.

But whether or not Block and Sibley accepted the government's authority over such matters, they still had to answer for the murder they had committed. Brought to trial, Block refused legal counsel and declared that the state of Alabama had no authority over her, since it had failed to officially rejoin the Union after the Civil War. Sibley, meanwhile, insisted that he could not be tried for murder since he had not fired the fatal shot. Both defendants also claimed that they had acted in self-defense, although eyewitnesses said different.

In the end, all of their arguments came to nothing. Both Sibley and Block were found guilty and sentenced to death. Lynda Block went to the electric chair on May 10, 2002. George Sibley followed on August 4, 2005.

Mark Stroman

It is not often that you hear a convicted killer claim that the murder he committed was his "patriotic duty." But that was the assertion made by Mark Stroman, after he was convicted and sentenced to death for the October 2001 slaying of gas station owner Vasudev Patel. According to Stroman, he had committed the murder as revenge for the 9/11 terrorist attacks.

The video footage obtained from the crime scene told a different story. It showed Stroman entering the convenience store attached to the gas station and demanding money from Patel at gunpoint. Before the man even had a chance to respond, Stroman pulled the trigger, hitting Patel in the chest. He then stepped over Patel and tried to open the register. Unable to do so, he threatened his mortally wounded victim with the gun. "Open the register or I'll kill you," he snarled. Patel, however, had already lapsed into unconsciousness. He would die before help arrived. By then, Stroman had fled, leaving behind the money he'd come to steal.

Stroman was apparently unaware that there was a video camera in the store. He would later tell a fellow inmate that he'd checked the place out three times before committing the robbery and hadn't seen any surveillance equipment. But the store was monitored and the video footage allowed police to get an immediate fix on Stroman. He was arrested within a day of the shooting, still carrying the .44-caliber handgun that had killed Vasudev Patel. Patel, as it turned out, was not his only victim.

On September 15, just four days after the 9/11 attacks, Stroman had walked into a convenience store in Dallas and gunned down Pakistani immigrant Waqar Hasan. Hasan had died at the scene. Six days later, Stroman had invaded another convenience store, this time shooting Raisuddin Bhuiuian, who survived the attack. In neither of these cases had Stroman attempted to rob the victims. As he proudly told officers, he had a grudge against people of Middle Eastern origin because of what had happened in New York and Washington. "Y'all people didn't do your job putting things right so I had to do it for you," he said, adding that he felt it was his "patriotic duty." Ironically, none of the men he'd shot were from the Middle East. All three were from the Indian subcontinent.

Mark Stroman is not unique in claiming revenge for September 11 as a motive. In the aftermath of those tragic events, there were several unprovoked attacks on innocent civilians. One notable case involved a serial killer named Larme Price who gunned down four Asian men between February and March 2003. The difference between Price and Stroman is that the former committed his crimes in New York, where the death penalty had been effectively ended in 1984. Stroman had committed his murders in Texas, the state that executes more killers than any other.

Thus it was that Mark Stroman was tried, found guilty and sentenced to death. Despite numerous petitions on his behalf (including one by his surviving victim, Raisuddin Bhuiuian) he was executed by lethal injection on April 5, 2002. Stroman maintained his patriotic motive to the end. "Even though I lay on this gurney, seconds away from my death, I am at total peace" he said in his final statement. "I'm still a proud American, Texas loud, Texas proud. God bless America. God bless everyone. Let's do this damn thing."

Robert Carter

On the evening of June 24, 1981, 17-year-old Robert Carter walked into a southeast Houston service station armed with a borrowed .38 Special. He surveyed the scene, taking in the position of security cameras and trying to keep his face hidden from them, while pretending to browse the aisles. Then, once he was alone in the store, he approached the clerk.

At 18, Sylvia Reyes was barely older than the would-be robber. Yet, in the next few moments, the fates of both these teenagers would be decided. Robert drew his weapon and demanded the contents of the register. Sylvia, offering no resistance, handed over just shy of $150. Robert could have taken the money and run. Instead, he fired a single shot, hitting the cashier in the face and killing her instantly.

It was a senseless murder and a poorly executed crime. After splitting the loot with some friends, Carter was left with just $37 for his trouble. He also, soon after, ended up in custody when one of those friends spoke out of turn and his words reached the ears of a police informant. Pressed about the murder, Carter soon buckled. He admitted to the shooting and to another, the gunning down of 63-year-old R. B. Scott, in a similar holdup just a few days earlier. In making that confession, Carter all but ended his own life as well.

Robert Carter had chosen a bad place to commit capital homicide. The state of Texas executes more murderers than any other in the nation, and Carter's case was about as open and shut as it gets. Brought before the courts, he entered a guilty plea, meaning that the trial went directly to the sentencing phase. That lasted no more than a few hours before the jury retired, returning just ten minutes later to recommend that Robert Carter be put to death.

Carter was shipped off to death row where he earned the nickname "Youngblood" due to his youth. He would remain there for nearly 16 years while his defenders filed appeals and clemency petitions, and there were submissions from the usual civil rights groups, Amnesty International, the ACLU, the NAACP. All of these were rejected. Robert Carter kept his date with the executioner on May 18, 1998, when he was put to death by lethal injection at the Huntsville Unit in Huntsville, Texas.

But should it have even come to this? Should more consideration have been given to the mitigating circumstances in this case? Perhaps, but the jury never got to hear that evidence.

Carter had suffered severe deprivation as a child and was regularly beaten with belts, clubs, and electrical cables. Serious head injuries were left untreated. As a result, the boy experienced seizures and fainting spells. He also developed mild mental retardation. And the injuries did not end in childhood. Just months before he killed Sylvia Reyes, Carter was shot himself, during an altercation with his brother. The bullet was later removed from his skull but no real assessment was done as to the damage it might have caused.

That damage is almost certain to have included impaired judgement. Because of it, two innocent people were needlessly gunned down and Robert Carter paid for their deaths with his own life.

George Hassell

George Hassell was born in Smithville, Texas, on July 4, 1888, the youngest of seven children. He grew up to be a giant of a man, a ne'er-do-good who got a girl pregnant in his teens, then promptly abandoned her and their unborn child. Thereafter, he began wandering, twice joining the Army and once the Navy, absconding on each occasion, and eventually serving a two-year prison term for desertion. He married six times, and that was quite aside from the many women he cohabitated with, living as man and wife.

One of those women was Marie Vogel, who Hassell met in Whittier, California, in 1916. Vogel had a young son, plus two orphaned children who she had adopted. Everything apparently went well with the relationship until Hassell told Marie that he had decided to enlist and join the fighting going on in Europe at the time. An argument then ensued during which Hassell grabbed Vogel by the throat and maintained his grip until Marie dropped like a limp rag doll at his feet. According to Hassell's later account, he then decided to kill the children, since there was now no one to care for them. The three infants (the youngest just a year old) were strangled in their beds. Their tiny bodies were then committed to the earth in the crawlspace of the house, along with their mother. Hassell then hit the road again, traveling to Oklahoma, Texas, and eventually to Louisiana.

It was while he was in New Orleans that Hassell received word from his sister-in-law, Susie. His brother had been killed in an accident at the family farm in Blair, Oklahoma. With a crop in the field, Susie desperately needed help. Could George come to her assistance? George said that he would, and before long, he'd taken his brother's place on the farm and also in Susie's bed. Eventually, he led his former sister-in-law to the altar and took responsibility for his eight nieces and nephews.

But Susie soon learned that George was nothing like her former husband. He was a deadbeat who enjoyed his booze and had an eye for other females. And he wasn't particularly worried about the age of his conquests. Shortly before the family moved to Farwell, Texas, in 1926, Susie became aware that George was sleeping with her 13-year-old daughter, Maudie. When she confronted him, George laughed it off but made no effort to deny that it was true.

The illicit relationship became a constant source of acrimony between George and Susie. On December 8, 1926, it eventually exploded into violence. Annoyed by his wife's constant badgering, Hassell picked up a hammer and beat her to death. He then took a straight razor and went to the room where the children were sleeping. Moving from bed to bed, he either slit their throats or strangled them to death.

Even Hassell's beloved Maudie was killed. Having completed the vile deed, he carried the bodies into the root cellar and buried them. He then hunkered down to await the return of Susie's oldest son, 21-year-old Alton, who'd been in town while Hassell was murdering the rest of his family. Alton was dispatched with a shotgun blast to the back of his head, then buried beside the rest of his family.

Had Hassell simply fled at that time, he might well have escaped justice. But he stayed behind to sell off the family's possessions, rousing the suspicions of neighbors. They, in turn, contacted the sheriff, who was unconvinced by Hassell's assertion that his family had moved to Oklahoma and that he would soon be joining them. That story was proven to be a lie once the police found recently disturbed ground in the root cellar and started uncovering the freshly butchered bodies. Then Hassell cracked and gave a three-word confession. "I did it," he said, barely batting an eye. He went on to describe the slaughter of his family, admitting also to the four murders he'd committed in California, a decade earlier.

George Hassell went on trial in Farwell, Texas, charged with nine counts of murder. Found guilty, he was condemned to death and then transported to Huntsville, Texas, to await execution. There he annoyed the other death row inmates with his constant boasts. "I'm not afraid to die," he told them. "The electric chair holds no more fear for me than a barber chair."

On February 2, 1928, the date finally arrived for Hassell to put his bravado to the test. In his final statement, he declared: "I would like to announce to the world that I am prepared to meet my God. Man does not understand it all, but God does." A short while later, three blasts of electricity were passed through Hassell's body, delivering the heartless killer to his deserved death.

John Taylor

The condemned man had chosen to die by firing squad, a method of execution rarely used in the U.S. but nonetheless available as an option in three states – Oklahoma, Idaho, and Utah. His reason, he said, was to embarrass the authorities. At precisely 12:00 a.m. on January 26, 1996, John Albert Taylor was led into the execution chamber at the State Prison in Draper, Utah. He was strapped into a chair by his hands and feet and a chin strap was fitted before the black hood was slipped over his head. Facing him from a distance of 23 feet were five riflemen, all of whom had volunteered for the task.

Each man was armed with an identical Winchester Model 94 rifle. Four were loaded with live ammunition, the fifth with a blank so that no man would ever know for certain if he had delivered a fatal shot. At 12:03 a.m., on the command of the warden, each of the riflemen brought his weapon into a firing position. Then, on the count of three, they fired, aiming for a white cloth target pinned over Taylor's heart. A dark patch of blood instantly welled up and darkened the cloth and the front of Taylor's navy blue shirt. A small amount of it spilled into a pan positioned under the chair's mesh seat. Four minutes later, a doctor declared John Taylor dead.

The crime that had brought John Taylor to this untimely end occurred on June 23, 1988, when he raped and killed 11-year-old Charla Nicole King inside her home in Washington Terrace, Utah. Horrific though that crime was, it was just the latest in a criminal career that had begun when Taylor was barely a teenager. That was when he stabbed and seriously injured his stepfather, earning him a stint in juvenile hall, a punishment that barely served to pause his lawless behavior. Released within two years, he began abusing drugs and sexually assaulting young girls, including his own sister, Laurie. That saw him committed to a program for young sex offenders – with limited success.

In 1977, the 18-year-old Taylor drew a four-year prison term for burglary and for carrying a concealed weapon. Released in December 1981, he drifted to Florida where he was arrested just three months later in Fort Lauderdale for burglary, armed robbery, and sexual assault. Those charges kept him behind bars until 1988, when he returned to Utah to live with his biological father.

At around 3:20 p.m. on June 23, 1988, Sherron King returned from work to her apartment in Washington Terrace. Usually, Sherron would be met at the door by her daughter Charla, but on this day, there was no greeting. The place was entirely quiet. Entering the home, Sherron called out her daughter's name but got no reply. She then conducted a quick search and found Charla lying on the floor in her bedroom, a nightgown wrapped around her head and her panties stuffed in her mouth. A frantic 911 call brought police and paramedics racing to the scene, but it was too late. Charla was dead, strangled with a telephone cord. She had also been raped. The little girl had been looking forward to celebrating her 12th birthday at an amusement park the next day.

Two days later, with the police having made very little progress in the case, an officer received a call from an anonymous tipster who offered up the name of John Albert Taylor. The caller turned out to be Laurie Galli, Taylor's sister, who had suffered so much abuse at his hands during her childhood. Fingerprints at the scene soon linked Taylor to the crime. It turned out that he'd been staying with another sister in the apartment complex where the murder was committed. He was arrested on June 28 in Ogden, Utah.

John Taylor went on trial for murder in November 1989, waiving his right to have his case heard before a jury. He denied murder, claiming that he'd left his fingerprints behind while burglarizing the King residence. But the forensics told a different story, and Taylor had also admitted the murder to a fellow inmate while awaiting trial. That admission would come back to haunt him. Found guilty of murder, he was sentenced to death, keeping his date with the firing squad on January 26, 1996.

FOOTNOTE: Utah banned execution by firing squad in 2004, although it was reinstated as an option in 2015. Idaho halted execution by firing squad in 2009. Due to the reluctance of drug companies to see their products used in executions, several other states are currently considering a return to the firing squad.

Wanda Jean Allen

Wanda Jean Allen was born in Oklahoma on August 17, 1959. The second of eight children, she was raised in poverty by an alcoholic mother and a father who abandoned the family after the birth of his last child. And those weren't the only problems Wanda had to deal with. At age 12, she was hit by a truck and knocked unconscious; at 15, she was stabbed in the left temple during a fight with another teenager. Both of these injuries left her with impaired brain function, specifically as relates to understanding cause and effect relationships. She also developed a tendency to behave irrationally when placed under stress. With a tested IQ of just 69 (indicative of mild mental retardation), she dropped out of high school at age 17. A short while later, she met Dedra Pettus, and the two of them became involved in a lesbian relationship.

On June 29, 1981, officers of the Oklahoma City Police Department were called to the apartment that Allen and Pettus shared. There, they found Dedra Pettus lying on the floor, dead from a bullet wound to the head. Allen readily admitted that she was the shooter but claimed that it had been an accident. According to her story, she'd gotten into an argument with a male friend of Pettus, and the man had then pulled a gun and shot at her. Allen had returned fire from about 30 feet away and Pettus had been caught in the crossfire.

The evidence, however, did not support Allen's story. It suggested that Pettus had been pistol-whipped prior to being shot at close range. The kill shot had certainly not been fired from 30 feet away, as Allen had claimed. Powder burns around the wound made a lie of that assertion. Nonetheless, prosecutors decided to cut a deal with Allen, and she was allowed to plead to manslaughter. That earned her a four-year stretch in the pen, of which she served just two before being released.

Allen's time behind bars had been mostly uneventful, but it had produced one significant outcome. It was during her prison stint that she met Gloria Jean Leathers. Like Allen, Leathers had been convicted of manslaughter after she'd stabbed a woman to death during an altercation outside a nightclub. In any case, Allen and Leathers became lovers. Once they were out on the streets again, they shacked up together. It was a turbulent and often violent relationship. Yet, against all odds, it endured for seven years until the afternoon of December 2, 1988, when Allen and Leathers got into a fist fight at a local grocery store and the police were called.

Officers soon arrived on the scene and, with some difficulty, they managed to separate the warring women. The officers then accompanied them back to their shared apartment and stood by while Leathers packed up her belongings and left. Her parting words to Allen were that she intended to bring charges of assault. That threat turned out to be a tragic mistake. When Leathers arrived at the Village Police Station in the company of her mother later that day, Allen was waiting. Leathers had barely stepped out of her mother's car when Allen walked up, drew a gun and fired a single shot, hitting Leathers in the stomach. Allen then fled the scene but was captured a short while later. She was initially charged with attempted murder, but that was upgraded when Gloria Leathers died in hospital three days later on December 5, 1988.

From the outset, prosecutors made it clear that they intended seeking the death penalty for Wanda Jean Allen. Allen's defense team countered by citing the victim's own history of violent behavior and insisting that their client had acted in self-defense. But that argument was deeply flawed. Leathers had been unarmed, and Allen had fired without provocation in the presence of an eyewitness. It was hardly a surprise when the jury rejected the self-defense argument and found Allen guilty of first-degree murder. She was then sentenced to death.

Wanda Jean Allen would spend 12 years on death row before her date with the executioner eventually rolled around. During the intervening years, there had been the usual appeals, as well as numerous pleas for clemency. All had been rejected.

On Thursday, January 11, 2001, Allen was rolled on a gurney into the execution chamber at Oklahoma State Penitentiary in McAlester. "Father, forgive them," she responded when asked if she had any final words. "They know not what they do." She then stuck her tongue out and smiled at her lawyer, Steve Presson. Moments later, the lethal drugs began to flow. Allen was pronounced dead at 9:21 p.m.

Earl Frederick

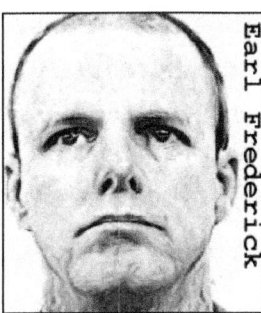

There had been a time when Earl Frederick Sr. had stood on the other side of the law, a time when he'd been an assistant police chief in Noble, Texas. Now, the former police officer lay strapped to a gurney at the Oklahoma State Penitentiary, ready to receive the flow of deadly chemicals that would dispatch him to the afterlife. Not that Frederick was denying culpability. He'd waived all appeals. Just a year earlier, he'd addressed a letter to the authorities in which he'd stated: "Mere words cannot begin to express the sorrow I feel over my actions. I am guilty of the crime, let there be no doubt of that."

The crime Frederick was referring to was a particularly heinous one. The victim, 41-year-old Bradford Lee Beck, was a disabled Vietnam War veteran who had befriended Frederick in November of 1989. Frederick, down on his luck, had accepted Beck's offer of a place to stay. The two had appeared to have a solid friendship, with Beck introducing Frederick to his friends and family as an old war buddy and saying that they'd spent time together in a VA hospital.

But within a week of Frederick moving in, both men were gone, and so too were Beck's clothes and valuables. Friends and family hoped that Beck had decided to go on a spur-of-the-moment road trip with his old buddy but thought that improbable given his health. He would not, in any case, have left without telling them. The more likely scenario was that he'd come to harm, probably at the hands of his re-found friend. That, tragically, proved to be an accurate assessment. Bradford Beck's decomposed corpse was found in a field near Midwest City, Oklahoma, in January 1990. He'd been bludgeoned to death, with the autopsy showing massive head trauma.

At the time of that discovery, Earl Frederick was already in custody, having been arrested on another murder charge. On November 19, just days after fleeing Oklahoma, he'd showed up in Texline, Texas. There, he'd murdered 77-year-old Sidney Fox during the course of a robbery. The elderly man was beaten to death with a hammer, then finished off with a shotgun blast to the face. Frederick was arrested in an Amarillo, Texas, bar, days later, still wearing the clothes he'd stolen from his first victim, Bradford Beck.

Had Frederick not been arrested when he was, it is highly likely that he would have gone on to become a serial killer. And like others of that ilk, he fell back on an old standby to justify his actions. It wasn't he who had committed the murders, he said, it was one of his many personalities, a malevolent entity named Jeff.

This defense has, of course, been tried before, most notably in the case of Hillside Strangler, Kenneth Bianchi. It failed then, and it failed again now. Frederick was extradited back to Oklahoma to stand trial for the murder of Bradford Beck. There he was convicted and sentenced to death. That conviction would later be overturned, but the retrial produced the same result, a guilty verdict and death penalty.

Earl Frederick had by that time decided anyway that he wanted to die. His wish was granted on July 30, 2002, when he was put to death by lethal injection.

David Alan Gore

In 1976, David Alan Gore and his cousin Fred Waterfield came up with an appalling plan. They were going to stalk, abduct, and rape women in their home town of Vero Beach, Florida. Fortunately, though, the cousins were particularly inept criminals, and all of their early targets escaped. When they did eventually succeed in capturing and sexually assaulting some unfortunate woman, they were promptly arrested. They only escaped conviction because the victim refused to testify. Shortly after, Waterfield left town, and the criminal partnership was broken.

Fast forward to 1981, and we find David Gore working as caretaker of a citrus plantation and patrolling the streets by night as an auxiliary sheriff's deputy. Waterfield was by now living in Orlando, but he still visited Gore regularly in Vero Beach. It was during one of these visits that he suggested that they resume their "hunts." Gore, after all, had the perfect cover – a sheriff's badge that would allow him to easily exert control over potential victims. Not only that, but he had access to a large plantation where they could bury the bodies. And there was little doubt that there would be bodies. Gore was adamant that they'd have to kill their victims. They couldn't run the risk of anyone testifying against them. Waterfield liked the idea so much that he offered Gore $1,000 for any pretty girl he managed to abduct.

On February 19, 1981, Gore spotted 17-year-old Ying Hua Ling and tricked her into his car, using his police badge. He then drove her home where he also took her mother into custody, saying that they were both being arrested for shoplifting. With the two women in handcuffs, he phoned Waterfield, then drove to the orchard where he took his time taunting the victims before raping both of them. When Waterfield eventually arrived, he too raped Ying Hua. Then it was time to follow through on part two of the plan, and it was agreed that Waterfield would strangle Ying Hua while Gore killed her mother. Mrs. Ling, however, was already dead. Gore had kept her tied to a tree during the ordeal and had knotted the rope too tightly around her throat. The bodies ended up buried in an orange grove.

Five months later, on July 15, Gore again employed his false arrest ruse, this time to abduct 35-year-old Judith Daley from Round Island Park. Waterfield was happy that Gore had delivered the blonde he had requested and paid the agreed-upon $1,000 for the pleasure of raping her. Afterward, Gore was left to dispose of the corpse. He would later testify that he'd "fed her to the alligators" in a swamp west of Interstate 95.

A week after the Daley murder, Gore tried to force a teenager into his vehicle but was accosted by her father who reported him to the Sheriff's Department. As a result, he was stripped of his badge, but that was soon the least of his problems. He was arrested soon after when he was caught hiding in a woman's car, armed with a pistol. That earned him a five-year prison term, although he served less than two. By the time he was paroled, Waterfield had moved back to Vero Beach, and the two started working together again. On May 21, they abducted, raped, and killed two 14-year-olds, Angelica Lavallee and Barbara Byer.

On July 26, 1983, Vero Beach authorities received a report of a man firing shots at a naked girl on a residential street. Officers rushed to the scene and found a car with blood dripping from its trunk. Inside lay the body of 17-year-old Lynn Elliott, a bullet lodged in her skull. Confronted by the police, David Gore meekly surrendered. A search of the house turned up a naked and terrified 14-year-old girl tied to the rafters in the attic. According to the girl, she and Elliott had been hitchhiking when Gore and another man had picked them up, threatened them with a gun, and then brought them to the house. There they were stripped, tied up and repeatedly raped. Elliott had managed to escape and had ended up being shot to death in the street.

Under interrogation, Gore quickly cracked, admitting to six murders and implicating his cousin. At his trial in March 1984, he was found guilty and sentenced to death. He was executed by lethal injection on April 12, 2012. Fred Waterfield, meanwhile, had been convicted of the Byer/Levallee murders and sentenced to two life terms.

Lonnie Johnson

Gunar Nelson Fulk, aged 16, and Leroy McCaffrey, aged 17, were friends who attended Magnolia High School in Tomball, a suburb of Houston, Texas. Fulk also worked part-time as a stock clerk at a grocery store. It was there that McCaffrey picked him up on the night of August 15, 1990. The boys then drove to another store to visit a friend, Tammy Durham. They were just about to leave when they were approached by a black man wearing cut-off jeans and a dirty t-shirt and holding a rolled up newspaper. He asked them for a ride, saying that his car had run out of gas some distance down the road. McCaffrey agreed to help him out. Through the window of the grocery store, Tammy Durham saw them drive off together in McCaffrey's pickup.

The following morning, Harris County police got a report of a body lying beside a rural road. A patrol car was diverted to the area and soon discovered the corpse of a young man, later identified as Gunar Fulk. He'd been shot three times in the head and once in the chest. About 350 feet away lay the body of Leroy McCaffrey, shot twice in the back. It appeared that he had tried to flee from the gunman but had been chased down and killed.

McCaffrey's pickup was also missing from the scene, and once detectives learned of the black man he'd given a ride to, a bulletin was issued on the truck and the suspect. Both, however, had already left the area. After shooting the boys, their killer, 23-year-old Lonnie Earl Johnson, had driven their pickup to Austin, Texas, to visit his girlfriend. He'd later abandoned the vehicle in a restaurant parking lot and sold the murder weapon to buy drugs. He was eventually arrested in San Marcos, Texas, on August 30, two weeks after the shootings.

Johnson made no attempt to deny that he had shot the boys. However, his version of events differed significantly from what detectives had inferred from the crime scene. According to Johnson, he'd acted in self-defense. He said that he'd been out jogging that night and had stopped outside the grocery store for a breather. There he was approached by the two boys and asked if he wanted a ride. Johnson had accepted, but just a short distance down the road, the truck had pulled over. Then the boys had forced him from the vehicle at gunpoint, racially abused him, and urinated on him. They'd told him he was going to die, leaving him with no option but to fight back. In the ensuing struggle, both boys had been shot and killed.

Johnson was still sticking to that story when the matter came to trial. "I am innocent by reason of self-defense," he said. "The only difference between me and James Byrd Jr. is that I lived." (James Byrd Jr. was an African-American man who was killed after being dragged behind a pickup truck in Jasper County in 1998. Three white men were convicted of the crime and two of them sentenced to death.)

But Johnson was being disingenuous in comparing himself to Byrd. In his case, the story simply did not match the facts. For starters, his claim that he'd been out jogging was ludicrous. Who goes out jogging during the early morning hours dressed in cut-off jeans and a dirty t-shirt?

Then there was his story about the boys pulling a gun on him. Neither McCaffrey nor Fulk owned a firearm. Johnson, however, had been spotted outside the grocery store holding a rolled-up newspaper which might easily have been used to conceal a weapon. In fact, the reason Tammy Durham had called the boys in the first place was because she'd spotted Johnson outside the store acting suspiciously. Why, if he'd acted in self-defense, had he run after one of the victims and shot him in the back? And why had he stolen the victim's truck?

There was also the matter of character. Both of the victims were high school students with impeccable disciplinary records. Johnson, on the other hand, had a long history of violence. At age 17, he'd been arrested for attacking his girlfriend with a brick. Another girlfriend testified that he'd punched her in the face and stolen her car. At the time of the murder, he was on probation, having been convicted of assaulting a female relative. He also had previous convictions for burglary and larceny. While in jail awaiting trial, he'd assaulted fellow inmates on three separate occasions, breaking a broom handle on the head of one of the men.

This was the kind of man who wanted the jury to believe that he'd been intimidated and abused by a couple of high school kids?

In the end, the jury didn't believe him. Johnson was found guilty and sentenced to death. He was executed by lethal injection on July 24, 2007, still protesting his innocence.

Cameron Willingham

It was a sight that neighbors of the Willingham family in Corsicana, Texas, would never forget. The Willinghams' home was on fire with three little girls, Amber, 2, and 1-year-old twins Karmon and Kameron, trapped inside. Yet here was the children's father, Cameron Willingham, ignoring their plight completely, pushing his car down the drive to keep it away from the flames.

Later, after firefighters had entered the home and brought out the bodies of the three dead girls, Willingham would claim that he'd made a heroic effort to enter the house and save his daughters. Yet, neighbors would paint that as a lie. They said that they had urged Willingham to rescue the children but that he'd remained crouched in the garden throughout, watching the house burn. A medical examination would confirm this. Willingham had almost no smoke in his lungs.

But by then, fire officials had already confirmed what most people suspected. The fire had been deliberately set, with an accelerant poured onto the floors and set alight. Who had started the blaze? The most likely suspect was Cameron Willingham himself. The man had showed no remorse over the deaths of his children. He'd seemed more concerned about his dartboard, complaining to a firefighter that it had been scorched in the blaze. And the day after the fire, December 24, 1991, he'd been seen sifting through the wreckage with his current wife (not the children's mother) laughing and joking while playing loud music on his car stereo.

These were not the acts of a grieving father who had lost his three baby girls two days before Christmas. But as detectives started looking into Willingham's background, they realized that he was no ordinary father. He was a man with a history of violence, convicted of numerous felonies and misdemeanors, both as a juvenile and as an adult. He was also known to be verbally and physically abusive toward his family. On one occasion, he'd so severely beaten his pregnant wife that she had suffered a miscarriage.

And there was an additional reason to suspect Willingham. The girls' lives had been insured, and he was already pushing the insurance company for his payout. By year's end, he would spend a sizable chunk of that cash on a brand new pickup.

Not that he'd have a whole lot of time to drive his new toy around. By early January, the forensic results were back, confirming fire investigators' initial suspicions. The fire had been deliberately set. On January 8, 1992, Cameron Willingham was taken into custody and charged with three counts of first-degree murder.

At his trial in August 1993, Willingham continued to claim that he was innocent. But the evidence was stacked up against him. There were the neighbors and several firefighters who described his callous, uncaring attitude during and after the fire; there were the forensic fire investigators who presented evidence that an accelerant had been used; there was an inmate who Willingham had given a jailhouse confession to. According to the snitch, Willingham had told him that he'd killed his daughters in order to conceal evidence of physical abuse on their bodies. Finally, there was a psychiatric expert who described Willingham as a sociopath and said that someone of his personality was beyond rehabilitation and would always pose a threat to society.

Then it was the turn of the defense, and they tried a classic reasonable doubt ploy by offering an alternate suspect. According to them, the fire had been set by the children's mother's current boyfriend. They could offer no evidence, much less a motive, to support their theory. In the end, the jury had a relatively straightforward task finding Willingham guilty. He was sentenced to death.

Cameron Willingham was executed by lethal injection on February 17, 2004. His final statement offered another glimpse into his narcissistic personality. After again protesting his innocence and assuring everyone present that he would soon be in heaven, he turned on his ex-wife, Stacy Kuykendall. "I hope you rot in hell, bitch," he spat.

Sterling Rault

Sterling Rault was an outgoing and affable family man who worked as an accountant for the Louisiana Energy & Development Corporation, a New Orleans-based gas pipeline company. He was married to his high school sweetheart and was the father of two children. He was also active in charitable events and was the organizer of the Jaycees Christmas Parade.

Jane Francioni worked in the same office as Rault, having joined the company in 1981, the same year that he had. A petite and pretty 21-year-old, she was close to her family and enjoyed nothing more than her regular lunch dates with her aunts and grandparents on Saturdays. She also had plans to return to college in pursuit of an accounting degree.

On the surface, these two individuals make unlikely protagonists in the dreadful events that were to come. But scratch a little deeper into Rault's history and some disquieting details emerge. Despite earning a respectable $28,000-a-year, Rault was a social climber who was dissatisfied with his lot in life. He'd left his previous job with the Masonite Corporation in Laurel, Mississippi, under a cloud over a $166,000 discrepancy in the company's accounts. No charges were brought, although it was noted that Rault had purchased a baronial residence while at Masonite, way above anything his salary would have afforded. He'd also installed a swimming pool and taken his family on expensive junkets to Disney World and San Francisco. Even more alarmingly, he'd been suspected in the attempted murder of the co-worker who had blown the whistle on him. The brakes on the man's car had been cut while he was attending church with his family.

Perhaps Rault was emboldened by the lack of sanction for his previous crimes. He had only been at his new job for a few months when he was at it again, forging the company president's name on checks and depositing them into a bogus bank account he'd set up. As Jane Francioni's supervisor, he also duped her into withdrawing cash from the account on his behalf.

But Rault had underestimated Jane. She was a bright girl, and she quickly picked up on the anomalies. When she did, she confronted Rault. She didn't want to cause trouble for him, she said, but if he continued, she'd have no option but to report him. Rault thanked her for coming to him first and promised that he would stay on the straight and narrow from now on. Unfortunately for Jane, he had no such intention. Instead he began plotting her death.

On the afternoon of March 1, 1982, Rault asked Jane for a ride to a class he was attending at Louisiana State's local campus. Jane, of course, agreed, but they'd only covered a short distance when Rault produced a gun and ordered her to drive to a quiet street on the city's east side. There, he savagely raped the young woman for over two hours before shooting her in the stomach and then slitting her throat. He then dragged her body from the car to a space between two dumpsters. There he poured gasoline over it and lit it on fire, no doubt hoping to destroy forensic evidence.

But Rault had miscalculated badly in starting the fire. A state trooper spotted the flames and came to investigate. Spotting Rault trying to flee beneath a highway overpass, he gave chase and soon had his man in custody. Rault was then brought in for questioning and offered a ludicrous story about two men in ski-masks who had kidnapped them and attacked Jane. He was still telling that story when the matter came to trial in October 1982. The jury found it no more believable than the police had.

Rault was convicted of first-degree murder and sentenced to death. While on death row, he reverted to being an exemplary citizen. He taught other inmates to read and write, he wrote articles for prison ministries, and he corresponded with dozens of inmates who got to hear his work on Christian radio broadcasts. Perhaps he thought that these good deeds might somehow persuade the authorities to offer clemency, but that would turn out to be a forlorn hope.

Sterling Rault died in the electric chair at the Louisiana State Prison on August 24, 1987. Right until the end, and in spite of the overwhelming evidence against him, he continued to maintain his innocence. "I would like the public to know that they are killing an innocent man," he said in his final statement. "I pray that God will forgive all those involved in this matter. I, personally, do not hold any animosity towards anyone."

Hans Schmidt

Born in the Bavarian city of Aschaffenburg, Germany in 1881, Hans Schmidt grew up with only one ambition in life. He wanted to be a priest, he'd tell anyone who would listen, repeating it so often that he acquired the nickname "Little Father" in his hometown. This, however, was no childish whim. Hans would eventually realize his ambition. In 1906, he was ordained to the Catholic priesthood in Mainz, Germany. Then, having achieved his lifelong dream, he went out of his way to ruin it.

Schmidt had barely begun his pastoral career when he developed a reputation for dishonesty. That would eventually culminate in a court case in 1909, when he stood accused of presenting forged educational credentials. An insanity plea at trial saved him from jail time but did not spare him a suspension from the church. With his reputation irreparably tarnished, he decided that a fresh start might be best for all. A short while later, he announced to his family that he was moving to America.

Schmidt's first posting in the U.S. was to Louisville, Kentucky. However, he was soon in conflict with another priest in that parish and ended up transferred to St. Boniface Church in New York City. He'd barely unpacked his bags in the Big Apple when he was involved in a fresh scandal, this time over a love affair with a pretty young housekeeper at the church named Anna Aumuller. When the church elders got to learn of the relationship, they sought to break the couple up by transferring Schmidt to another congregation. Schmidt, however, was not about to give up his lover that easily. He set Anna up in an apartment near his new diocese and the affair continued. And, perhaps inevitably, Anna fell pregnant.

Schmidt seems to have genuinely cared for Anna. But her pregnancy put him in a difficult position. As a staunch Catholic, Anna would never countenance an abortion, which left Schmidt with two options. He could either deny that he was the father (and hope that the church believed him) or he could quit his position and marry Anna. In the end, he decided on a third way. He decided to murder the mother of his unborn child.

On August 31, 1913, Schmidt stopped off at a local hardware store and purchased a handsaw and a large knife. Two days later, he crept into Anna's apartment in the early morning hours and slashed her throat. He then dissected her body, wrapped the sections in paper and dumped them into the Hudson River.

On September 5, 1913, two young men were walking along the New Jersey bank of the Hudson when they spotted a package in the water. Curious as to what it contained, they hauled it ashore and opened it. They instantly wished they hadn't. Inside was the headless trunk of a woman.

Over the days that followed, several more body parts washed up on the riverbank. These were taken to the city morgue where a pathologist determined that they were from a young woman who had been pregnant at the time of her death. There was only one clue to her identity. Some of the body parts had been contained in a pillow case bearing a crudely embroidered letter "A."

That pillowcase would form the backbone of the investigation. First, detectives traced its manufacturer and learned that the item in question had been delivered to a Manhattan apartment. The landlord there informed him that the unit was occupied by a young woman named Anna Aumuller, who worked as a housekeeper at St. Boniface Church. Calling on the church, the investigators learned that Anna had last showed up for work on August 31. They were also given the name of Father Hans Schmidt, discreetly described as "a friend of Anna Aumuller."

Father Schmidt was clearly thrown by the arrival of two NYPD detectives at his door, but he quickly regained his composure. Under questioning, he admitted that he and Anna were friends but insisted that their relationship was "entirely innocent." He also claimed that he knew nothing of her whereabouts.

The detectives, though, were unconvinced. They continued probing and eventually Hans Schmidt cracked. Sobbing pitifully, he admitted that he and Anna had been involved in a sexual relationship and that he'd killed her after she fell pregnant. He also claimed that he'd been deeply in love with her. Asked why he'd then murdered Anna, Schmidt could offer only a bizarre explanation. "Sacrifices should be consummated in blood," he said.

Father Hans Schmidt went on trial for murder on December 7, 1913. He entered an insanity plea that would ultimately be rejected by the jury. Found guilty of murder on February 5, 1914, he was sentenced to death, that sentence eventually carried out in the electric chair at Sing Sing two years later. Father Schmidt remains the only Roman Catholic priest to be executed in the United States.

Thomas J. Grasso

Seldom has a condemned man made a more flippant final statement. Thomas Grasso, the savage murderer of two elderly victims, chose to voice his displeasure about the last meal he'd requested. "I did not get my Spaghetti-O's," he whined. "I got spaghetti. I want the press to know this."

The path that had led Grasso to this point – strapped to a gurney in the execution chamber at the Oklahoma State Penitentiary, complaining about culinary arrangements – had begun years earlier. Grasso already had a long criminal record on the fateful Christmas Eve in 1990 when he showed up at the Tulsa, Oklahoma, home of 87-year-old Hilda Johnson. The elderly woman lived alone but had nonetheless decorated her living room with a tree, strung with fairy lights. Those self-same lights would be put to deadly use by the killer. He looped them around Mrs. Johnson's neck and pulled them tight, throttling the life out of her. Then, just to be sure, he took a clothes iron and battered her head in. His take from this wanton act of murder? $12 and an ancient TV set.

Six months later, on July 3, 1991, Grasso was living in a Staten Island boarding house when he entered the room of fellow resident, Leslie Holtz. The 81-year-old man was savagely beaten and strangled to death, whereupon Grasso robbed him of his meager possessions and fled. He didn't get far, though. Just two weeks later, he was taken into custody and charged with murder. He made no attempt to deny it. At the subsequent trial, he entered a guilty plea and asked to be put to death. That request, unfortunately, could not be granted. New York had no death penalty on its statute books. Grasso got 20-years-to-life instead.

But by now, Oklahoma had linked Grasso to the murder of Hilda Johnson and was pushing for his extradition. Oklahoma does, of course, put convicted murderers to death, and that was perhaps why New York governor, Mario Cuomo, refused. Cuomo was a staunch opponent of capital punishment. Oklahoma could have Grasso, he said, after Grasso had served the 20 years he owed the people of New York.

And so, a tense custody battle ensued between the two states, with the object of their feud weighing in by expressing his eagerness to be shipped off to Oklahoma and put to death. The impasse was only resolved after Cuomo was ousted from office by Republican George E. Pataki, who'd swept into power on a strong law enforcement platform. Part of his pledge had been a commitment to restore the death penalty in New York, and the Grasso case had been mentioned frequently in his campaign speeches. He'd even delivered one of those speeches from outside the boarding house where Leslie Holtz had been killed.

So it was that, in January 1995, just eleven days after Governor Pataki took office, the order was signed. Thomas Grasso was going back to Oklahoma where certain death awaited him. Grasso had no problem with that. After pleading guilty to murder and accepting the inevitable death penalty, he waived all appeals, meaning that his execution could proceed within 60 days.

Thomas J. Grasso was put to death by lethal injection on March 20, 1995. The execution went off smoothly, even if the condemned man went to his death disgruntled at the lack of canned spaghetti.

Newton Anderson

On the afternoon of March 4, 1999, firefighters were called to the residence of Frank and Bertha Cobb near Tyler, Texas, after a neighbor noticed smoke billowing from the residence. The firemen soon had the blaze under control, but not before they'd made a couple of horrific discoveries. The elderly couple had both been murdered. Frank, 71, lay in the kitchen, his hands bound, his head and chest obliterated by shotgun blasts fired at close range. His 65-year-old wife, Bertha, was lying on the floor of the living room. She too, had been shot in the head, but the killer had also pulled a length of electrical cord tightly around her throat in an apparent attempt to strangle her. She was also nude from the waist down, suggesting a sexual assault. The presence of semen, found at the subsequent autopsy, would confirm this initial impression.

It was a brutal crime and one the police in Smith County were desperate to solve. Fortunately, the killer had been less than clever in his efforts to avoid detection. The fire had not wrought the damaged he had hoped, and police were able to determine that several items had been stolen from the house. Also missing was the couple's maroon Cadillac, and it was that which would provide the police with their first break in the case. A neighbor had seen a young man with red hair driving away from the crime scene in the vehicle.

Although the police didn't have the identity of that man yet, he was no stranger to law enforcement. He was a lowlife and perpetual criminal named Newton Anderson, recently released from a four-year stretch for burglary. Prior to that, he'd been in and out of prison on a catalog of offenses, usually burglary and car theft. He also had somewhat of a reputation as an escape artist and had acquired the nickname "Hacksaw Red" after an attempt to saw through the bars of his cell. Frank and Bertha Cobb had had the misfortune of encountering Hacksaw Red while he was in the process of burglarizing their home. They'd paid for it with their lives.

As yet, though, the police had not been able to put a name to the red-headed suspect. On the same afternoon that he'd so cold-bloodedly murdered the Cobbs, Anderson had pulled into the trailer park where he lived with his nephew and asked for help unloading items from the maroon Cadillac he was driving. Those items included a duffel bag and a suitcase stuffed with clothing, some toiletry items, and an oscillating fan. Anderson then drove away in the car, returning a short while later on foot and telling his nephew that he'd had to get rid of the vehicle because it was "hot." He then asked his niece and her boyfriend for a ride to a Dallas nightclub, offering them $80 for making the trip. They thought this unusual, since Anderson was usually broke. Nonetheless, they agreed to take him, and Anderson continued to spend lavishly throughout the evening.

What Anderson did not know was that he was enjoying his last night of freedom. On the evening of the murder, the police found Frank Cobbs' stolen Cadillac, hidden behind an abandoned building. Then a volunteer fireman came forward to say that he had seen Anderson walking along the highway in the vicinity of the abandoned car that very afternoon. The man knew Anderson and so was able to give his name to the authorities.

Newton Anderson was arrested the following day, still in possession of some of the cash he'd stolen from his victims. A search of his trailer then turned up the stolen items while an examination of the Cadillac produced a forensic link to Cobb. DNA lifted from the semen Anderson had left on Bertha Cobb provided the final piece. It was one of the easier murder inquiries the Smith County police had had to conduct and one of the easiest cases to prove in court.

Found guilty on two counts of capital murder, Newton Anderson was sentenced to death. He was executed by lethal injection on February 22, 2007.

Bennie Demps

It's not often that you get a second chance on death row. But Bennie Demps had been handed just such an opportunity in 1972. Sentenced to die for the murders of R.N. Brinkworth and Celia Puhlick in 1971, Demps had been reprieved a year later when the U.S. Supreme Court handed down its landmark Furman v. Georgia ruling, commuting all outstanding death penalties to life in prison.

The crime that had landed Demps on death row in the first place had occurred after a heist in which Demps and an accomplice, Jackie Hardie, stole a safe. The thieves had then driven to an orange grove in Lake County, Florida, where they had attempted to crack the combination. While they were doing so, estate agent R.N. Brinkworth arrived to show the property to Connecticut couple, Celia and Nicholas Puhlick, who were looking to purchase it as a retirement home. It was to their eternal detriment that they happened to stumble upon Demps and Hardie.

The robbers ordered Brinkworth and the Puhlicks into the trunk of their car. While deciding what to do with them, the trio tried to escape, and Demps and Hardie opened fire, killing Celia Puhlick and R.N. Brinkworth and severely injuring Nicholas Puhlick. He would survive to identify the killers and to testify at their trial. Hardie would later die in jail. Demps, meanwhile, would develop a reputation as one of the most troublesome inmates in the Florida prison system, racking up numerous citations for fighting and, on one occasion, nearly blinding another inmate by throwing boiling water in his face.

Much of Demps' violent activity centered around a prison gang called "Perjury Incorporated," a collective self-appointed to root out inmate informants. On September 7, 1976, three of the gang – Demps, James Jackson and Harry Mungin – homed in on inmate Alfred Sturgis who they suspected of passing information to the authorities. While Mungin stood in the doorway of Sturgis' cell and kept watch, Demps and Jackson entered. One of them (reportedly Demps) then held Sturgis down, while the other (Jackson) stabbed him repeatedly with a prison shank. The threesome then fled before guards could arrive.

But Sturgis wasn't dead. He was found with multiple deep stab wounds but still breathing. While being transported to the hospital, he was able to name his attackers. When he died later that night, Demps, Jackson and Mungin were arrested and charged with murder.

And if the timing of Demps' earlier murders had turned out fortuitously for him, his timing had deserted him the second time around. The State of Florida had re-instated the death penalty just two months earlier, and Bennie Demps would be one of the first prisoners to whom it was applied.

Demps would not go quietly to his death. He lodged every motion available to him and leveled accusations of corruption at the prosecutor and institutionalized racism at the prison system. In the meanwhile, his wife Tracey, a Canadian woman who he'd married in a death row ceremony in 1999, was trying to drum up support on the outside, claiming that Demps had been framed.

In the end, it was all to no avail. Demps had cheated the executioner the first time around, but there would be no repeat performance. He was put to death by lethal injection on June 7, 2000. Harry Mungin and James Jackson, Demps' co-accused in the Sturgis murder, were both given life sentences.

Charles Anthony Boyd

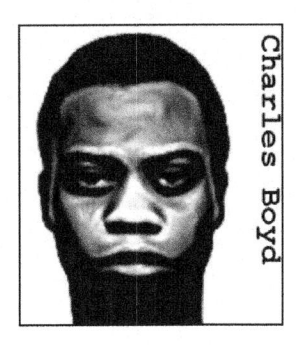

Over a ten-month period, from July 1986 to April 1987, three unusual murders occurred at the Woodstock apartment complex in northeast Dallas. In a series that the media dubbed "The Bathroom Slayings," the victims were strangled and left submerged in their bathtubs. Each of the young women had been sexually assaulted. Two had also been stabbed.

The first of these horrendous crimes came to light in July 1987 when the decomposed corpse of 37-year-old waitress, Tippawan Nakusan, was found stabbed and choked to death in her bathtub. The body was badly bloated, and it was estimated that it had been in the water for two weeks before the smell emanating from the apartment led to its discovery. Despite the chaotic nature of the crime scene, very little evidence had been left behind. Investigators fully believed that it was an isolated incident. They were wrong.

That September, another murder occurred at the Woodstock, so similar to the first that it could only have been committed by the same person. Lashun Chappell Thomas, a 22-year-old nursing aide, was found fatally stabbed in her bathtub. She'd also been strangled and sexually assaulted. Again there was nothing at the scene which might have provided a clue to the killer's identity.

And the police also got no result from the hours of legwork they put in, going door to door and questioning terrified residents. No one had seen or heard anything unusual, and none of the residents responded in a way that the detectives found suspicious. Eventually the investigation had to be wound down with the case no nearer to being resolved.

Six months passed. Then, on April 13, 1988, the killer struck again. Twenty-one-year-old Mary Mulligan was a recent graduate of Texas Tech University who had moved to Dallas to take a job as a management trainee with a local bank. On the day of her death, she'd stayed home with a sprained ankle. However, when she failed to answer her phone on April 14, her boyfriend called on the apartment and found her dead in the tub. She'd been strangled.

This time, though, there was a lead. Several items of jewelry were missing, and a bulletin to local pawnshops soon brought results. An ex-con named Charlie Boyd tried to hock some of the stolen items and was taken into custody. Boyd, who had only recently been paroled from a five-year prison stretch for burglary and rape, worked as a night janitor in another building. But he lived at the Woodstock apartments with his brother and could be connected to all of the victims. Mary Mulligan lived just across the hall from him, while Tippawan Nakusan occupied the apartment above. And Boyd had, of course, been found in possession of Mary Mulligan's jewelry.

But despite the strong circumstantial case against him, Boyd initially denied involvement in the murders. It would take sustained and skillful interrogation before he eventually cracked and admitted killing the three women.

Charles Boyd was charged with all three murders but would only stand trial for killing Mary Mulligan. At that trial, his defense attorney introduced the quite ludicrous motion that the charge should be reduced to voluntary manslaughter because, according to Boyd, Mulligan had angered him by calling him a name. Unsurprisingly, the motion was turned down. Then the defense tried another tack. Boyd's attorney contended that his client had an IQ of just 67, making him borderline retarded and therefore not responsible for his actions. This, too, was rejected.

In the end, it took just ten minutes for the jury to deliver a verdict of guilty. The judge then pronounced sentence of death. Charles Boyd was executed by lethal injection on August 5, 1999.

Carl Eugene Kelly

It was the early morning hours of September 2, 1980, and Carl Kelly and his associate Thomas Graves were cruising the streets of Waco, Texas, looking for someone to rob. Finding no convenient victims, the men decided to hold up a 7-Eleven, where the only employee at that hour was clerk, Steven Pryor. Pryor willingly handed over the contents of the register when Kelly demanded it at gunpoint. However, the robber expressed his disgust when the take amounted to just $30. He then marched Pryor out into the parking lot where there were two vehicles, one of which was Pryor's brown Camaro.

Also in the 7-Eleven parking lot at that time was a homeless man by the name of David Wade Riley. Riley had the massive misfortune of having crept into Steven Pryor's car for a few hours' sleep earlier in the evening. As a result, he found himself abducted, along with the store clerk. The men were driven to Cameron Park where their abductors debated for a while over what to do with them. Then, without warning, they opened fire, shooting both men and killing them instantly. Then they dragged the bodies to the edge of a 60-foot drop and threw them into the ravine below.

Unbeknownst to Kelly and Graves, Stephen Pryor's disappearance had already been noted. A customer had arrived at the store at around 4:15 a.m., just in time to see Pryor being marched to his car. The woman had then entered the store and found it unattended. She was about to call the police when Ed Torres, an off-duty policeman, entered the store. It was he who called it in.

Before long the 7-Eleven and its parking lot had been cordoned off as a crime scene. Soon a sizable crowd had gathered. In the midst of all this, the brown Camaro that pulled up over the road went almost unnoticed.

Kelly and Graves had returned to the crime scene so that Kelly could pick up his car. Seeing the crowd gathered outside the 7-Eleven and the police cars parked nearby, Kelly instructed his partner to drop him off, saying they'd meet up later. Graves then drove off in the Camaro while Kelly walked casually across the road and asked a police officer if he could retrieve his vehicle. The officer immediately noticed blood on Kelly's clothes and asked him about it. Kelly said that he'd been in a fight early in the evening. He also mentioned, without being asked, that he'd been in the store earlier, "buying a Slurpee." He was then allowed to get into his vehicle and leave, even recruiting members of the crowd to give him a push start.

Kelly's partner was not as fortunate in avoiding the law, however. An all-points bulletin had been issued on the missing Camaro, and Graves was pulled over just outside of Hillsboro at around 6 a.m. Inside the car, officers found two revolvers, bloodstained towels, and a rucksack containing clothes and prescription bottles in the name of David Wade Riley. They also found a wallet containing Carl Kelly's driver's license. That put Kelly firmly in the frame, and at 10:00 a.m. that morning, officers arrived at his place of work and took him into custody.

Thomas Graves quickly cracked under interrogation and confessed that both he and Kelly had fired at the victims. That same morning, he led officers to the bodies. He later struck a deal and agreed to plead guilty in order to avoid the death penalty. Kelly, meanwhile, admitted to being present when Pryor and Graves were shot but denied firing at them. According to him, Graves had been the sole shooter. Ballistics would prove that assertion to be a lie.

Offered the same deal as his co-accused, Kelly turned it down, saying that he'd take his chances at trial. That turned out to be a bad move. He was found guilty and sentenced to death. He was executed by lethal injection on August 22, 1993.

William Woratzeck

It was a savage murder, perpetrated against a woman who was both physically and mentally disabled. On the night of March 6, 1980, someone broke into the trailer occupied by 36-year-old Linda Louise Leslie at a mobile home park in Casa Grande, Arizona. Linda, who suffered from Huntington's chorea and had the mental capacity of a 15-year-old, was helpless against a brutal attack. She was beaten with a hammer, stabbed with a large kitchen knife, and then strangled to death with such force that the bones in her neck were fractured. The killer then stole $107 from her purse and lit the trailer on fire in an apparent effort to destroy evidence.

At first, investigators thought that this was a straightforward robbery/homicide, perpetrated by someone who had wanted to kill Linda Leslie for her meager possessions. But as detectives delved deeper into the case, they uncovered evidence of a strained relationship between Linda's family and her landlord, 35-year-old William Woratzeck.

Woratzeck owned the trailer that Linda was living in, but the trailer park belonged to Linda's aunt. He'd recently struck a deal to buy the place, leading to a two-tier arrangement. Linda paid rent to Woratzeck while he, in turn, paid installments to her family for the purchase of the park. When he'd fallen behind in his payments, Linda's family had stopped paying her rent, something that apparently annoyed Woratzeck.

But was it motive enough for murder? The police seemed to think so, because they brought Woratzeck in for questioning and then obtained a search warrant for his residence. Several items of clothing were taken in for analysis. On them, the police lab found specks of blood consistent with Linda Leslie's blood type. There were also carpet fibers which were matched to those inside Linda's home. Those, at least, could be explained away. Woratzeck was, after all, the murdered woman's landlord.

To investigators, though, William Woratzeck was their man. He was arrested and charged with murder. In response, Woratzeck accused the police of a cover-up. He said that he and Linda had been involved in a sexual relationship and claimed that he had also introduced other men to Linda for sex. Any of those men could have killed her and, according to Woratzeck, one of them was a senior Casa Grande police officer. He wasn't claiming that this officer was the killer, he said, only that the police did not want their colleague's indiscretions exposed and had therefore decided to pin the murder on a convenient fall guy.

It was a bold claim but one for which Woratzeck could offer no proof. Even his own lawyers did not believe that there was validity to the conspiracy theory, although they made it clear that the police efforts to solve the crime had been inadequate. They had focused their entire investigation on Woratzeck, not even bothering to look for other potential suspects.

The defense had a point. The case was circumstantial at best, sketchy at worst. It was, however, enough to convince the jury. They found Woratzeck guilty of murder and recommended the death penalty. Woratzeck would spend nigh on two decades fighting those decisions. Ultimately, his efforts would be in vain.

William Woratzeck was put to death by lethal injection on June 25, 1997. He continued to assert his innocence right until the end, declaring in his final statement: "I want the state of Arizona to know they are executing an innocent man. Tell my wife I love her."

Jason Getsy

In 1992, 17-year-old Jason Getsy was convicted of negligent homicide after a friend was killed while he and Getsy were playing Russian Roulette. Getsy served no jail time for that offense, nor did he appear to learn anything from the experience. Within three years, he'd be involved in another shooting, this time a deliberate act of murder which would land him on death row.

The murder that would end in Getsy's execution resulted from a dispute over, of all things, a landscaping business. Charles Serafino operated the business in Hubbard, Ohio, and John Santine wanted a piece of the action, which Serafino was happy to sell to him, accepting $2,500 in payment. A short while after that deal was struck, Serafino was sent back to prison for violating the conditions of his parole, and Santine attempted to take over the business. That resulted in Serafino's family filing a civil suit against him and thus sowing the seeds of a bitter dispute. After Serafino was released from prison, things became so heated that Santine started casting around for a hitman to eliminate his rival. It was

20-year-old high school dropout Getsy that answered the call, offering to do the job for $5,000 in cash.

At around 1:00 a.m. on the morning of July 7, 1995, Getsy and two accomplices, Ben Hudach and Richard McNulty, entered the Serafino residence. Getsy was armed with a pistol, one of the other men with a shotgun, which he used to blow out the lock on a side door. Awakened by the ruckus, Charles Serafino went to investigate and found himself confronted by a gun-wielding assailant who started firing immediately. Serafino was shot seven times, one of the bullets hitting him in the face. Miraculously, he would survive. His mother, Ann, was not so fortunate. She had also gotten out of bed to see what the noise was about. She ended up shot twice, once in the chest and once in the head. She died at the scene. By the time the police arrived, the assailants had fled.

Unfortunately for Getsy and everyone involved in the murder-for-hire scheme, John Santine was a loud mouth. He had spoken openly about having Serafino killed and had even confided in one acquaintance that Serafino was "bought and paid for." As soon as the police heard of those comments, Santine and his accomplices were arrested. Under interrogation, Getsy admitted shooting Charles and Ann Serafino but denied that he had done it for money. According to him, he'd carried out the hit because he was afraid of Santine, who was reputed to have mob connections.

The distinction was an important one because Ohio's statutes carry the death sentence for murder-for-hire killings. Aggravated murder charges would see Getsy potentially sentenced to life in prison; capital charges would see him sentenced to death. The prosecutor opted for capital charges.

In truth, Getsy's defense was always going to be a hard sell, especially after several witnesses testified that Getsy had boasted about killing Ann Serafino. It was no surprise when the jury found him guilty of capital murder with no recommendation of mercy. Of Getsy's accomplices, Ben Hudach got 20 years and Richard McNulty 30 years. John Santine, the mastermind behind the murder plot got life in prison with parole eligibility in 20 years.

Jason Getsy was put to death by lethal injection on August 18, 2009. In the run-up to his execution, the Ohio Parole Board had recommended that Gov. Ted Strickland grant clemency to Getsy, partly because ringleader John Santine had not been sentenced to death. Strickland rejected that appeal, saying that Getsy's culpability was not affected by Santine's sentence.

Arthur Waite

Born in rural Michigan in 1889, Arthur Warren Waite was raised in a poor sharecropping family. However, he was blessed with a sharp intellect, something that carried him through his schooling as a perpetual overachiever and saw him accepted into dentistry school after graduation. While enrolled there in 1908, he began dating a homely young woman named Clara Peck, whose father, John E. Peck, was a self-made millionaire. The Pecks counted themselves among the social elite, and the ambitious Waite was determined to insinuate himself into that circle.

There were a few things, however, that the Pecks did not know about their prospective son-in-law. They did not know, for example, that he was a serial philanderer with a string of affairs behind him; they did not know that he was a habitual liar; they did not know that his interest in Clara was financial rather than romantic. Arthur Waite had his eye on the Waite fortune. Part one of his plan was to marry Clara.

Just as Waite was about to make his move, however, a serious problem arose. He was caught plagiarizing another student's work and threatened with expulsion from school. Rather than face that ignonimity, he quit. Thereafter, he concocted an elaborate cover story, telling Clara that he'd been invited to study at Glasgow University's renowned dentistry school and would have to put their wedding plans on hold. He then gained admission to the school using fraudulent credentials and eventually obtained a master's degree there. Then, after a two-year spell in South Africa, he returned to Michigan where Clara was still patiently waiting. They were married soon after, settling in New York City where Waite established a dental practice.

In 1915, Waite enrolled as a private student at Cornell Medical School. His interest was in bacteriology, a strange field of study for a dentist, but one that gave him access to some of the deadliest pathogens available, including typhoid, cholera, diphtheria, tuberculosis, and anthrax.

In late 1915, Clara Waite's mother traveled to New York to spend some time with her daughter and son-in-law. She'd barely unpacked when she came down with a severe cold and had to be confined to bed. Then Dr. Waite stepped in and insisted on taking responsibility for her care. He brought her meals, massaged her feet, read to her, even crooned a few tunes in a passable baritone. But most of all, he attended to her medical needs, prescribing a nasal spray which, he said, would facilitate a swift recovery.

Hannah Peck died on January 30, 1916, her death attributed to natural causes. What the medical examiner could not have known was that the nasal spray given to her by Dr. Waite had contained a deadly blend of diphtheria and anthrax.

John Peck was devastated by the untimely death of his beloved wife. So much so, that he, himself, fell deathly ill within two months. Again, Dr. Waite stepped into the breach, offering care and medical advice while at the same time exposing his father-in-law to a catalog of pathogens, including tuberculosis, anthrax, and diphtheria. Peck, however, was tougher than his wife had been. When even a lethal dose of arsenic failed to kill him, Waite was forced to take desperate measures. He eventually killed Peck by chloroforming him and then suffocating him with a pillow.

But Waite had overstepped by murdering both of his wife's parents within such a short space of time. John Peck's son, Percy, had never been a big fan of Waite and was convinced that he was somehow involved in the deaths. Then, on the day of his father's memorial service, Percy received a tersely worded note which seemed to back up his suspicions. It consisted of just six words: "Stop funeral. Demand autopsy. Suspicions aroused." It was signed "K. Adams."

Percy immediately took this note to his local precinct where he handed it over to a detective and confided his belief that Waite had murdered his parents. Officers were then dispatched to question Waite but found him lying unconscious at his dental practice. He'd swallowed a handful of pills and may well have died had the officers not arrived when they did.

Waite was rushed to Bellevue Hospital where he would eventually make a full recovery. In the meanwhile, an autopsy had been carried out on John Peck's body and turned up evidence of arsenic poison. When vials of the same poison were found hidden at Waite's dental practice, he was arrested and charged with two counts of capital murder.

Arthur Warren Waite was brought to trial in May 1916. He entered an insanity plea, claiming that he'd received instructions to kill from a long-dead Egyptian pharaoh. When this, quite ludicrous, story was rejected by the jury, there could be only one outcome. Found guilty on two counts of murder, Waite was sentenced to death. He died in the electric chair at Sing Sing on May 24, 1917.

Mark Hopkinson

There had been a time when Mark Hopkinson was the golden boy of Fort Bridger, Wyoming, a football star who had earned himself a scholarship to the University of Arizona. But Mark had suffered an injury that had put an end to his college football career. And shortly thereafter, he'd been arrested on drugs charges and sent to federal prison. He'd served four years before being released. Thereafter, he'd returned to Wyoming and walked straight into the middle of a water rights dispute.

The argument centered on a trailer court that Mark's father, Joe, had built, cutting off a stream that fed the neighboring property, occupied by the Roitz family. They had hired a lawyer, Vincent Vehar, to challenge the action in court. Matters turned violent in May 1976, when Mark and Joe assaulted 55-year-old Frank Roitz, hitting him with a hammer. That had seen Vince Vehar pressing County Attorney Jim Phillips to bring charges. Phillips, who also happened to be Joe Hopkinson's lawyer, declined to do so. He did, however, warn the Hopkinsons about their future conduct.

The impasse did not last long. Soon there was another dispute, this time involving the Bridger Valley Water Board. Joe Hopkinson had approached the Board to hook up water and sewage to his new trailer court. Once the work was done, however, he refused to pay. When the Board insisted, several of its members received visits from Mark, threatening violence. Again it was Vincent Vehar who was hired to stand against him and his father.

But Mark Hopkinson was not the kind of man to sit around waiting for his day in court. In late 1976, he attempted to hire someone to kill Vincent Vehar. When the would-be assassin shirked, he tried another approach, attempting to bribe one of the Water Board members to switch sides. That also failed. Shortly afterward, Hopkinson turned to criminal associates, Jeff Green and Mike Hickey, for a solution.

Over the next four months, the trio discussed various ways of killing Vehar, eventually deciding on the unlikely solution of planting a bomb in the basement of his house in Evanston. Hickey was happy to volunteer for the job, suggesting that the going rate was $2,000. Hopkinson agreed to the price, provided the bombing was carried out before August 9, the day he and his father were due in court. Hickey said that he'd do it on Saturday, August 6.

On the night in question, Hickey visited several bars and got seriously drunk. This, however, would prove no impediment to him carrying out his part of the plot. The bomb was planted and exploded on schedule at 3:35 a.m., destroying the house. Vincent

Vehar, his wife Beverly, and his 15-year-old son John were all killed.

Since everyone knew about the bad blood between Mark Hopkinson and Vincent Vehar, Hopkinson was an obvious suspect. He, of course, had anticipated this and made sure that he had a cast-iron alibi. With no physical evidence connecting him to the bombing, there was little the police could do.

Hopkinson might well have gotten away scot-free if one of his accomplices, Jeff Green, had not decided to speak to the police. Although Green's testimony was deemed insufficient to support murder charges, it was enough to bring charges of conspiracy to commit murder. At the subsequent trial, Hickey was acquitted while Hopkinson was convicted and sent to a minimum security federal prison in Lompoc, California to serve his time. From there, he began plotting to kill the man who had informed on him.

Jeff Green was found shot to death beside Interstate 80 in May 1979. He had also been tortured, with more than 140 burn marks on his body. And perhaps it was the torture which spooked Mike Hickey. Shortly after, he contacted the authorities and asked for a deal. He would testify against Hopkinson in the Vehar bombing. In exchange, he wanted immunity from prosecution. He would, however, admit to another crime, the murder of a 15-year-old girl in which he'd long been a suspect. For that murder, he'd accept a 25-year prison sentence. With nothing else to go on, the county prosecutor agreed.

Mark Hopkinson would be convicted in separate trials of both the Vehar and Green murders. Although he did not physically carry out any of the killings, choosing instead to get others to do his dirty work, the jury decided that his role was enough justification for the death penalty. Hopkinson was executed by lethal injection on January 22, 1992, and is the only inmate be put to death by the state of Wyoming since the 1960s. His final words were, "They have killed an innocent man."

Will Lockett

At around 7:45 am on Wednesday, February 4, 1920, a farmer named Speed Collins was walking on his land in Fayette County, Kansas, when he came across a school satchel. Thinking that one of the students may have dropped it, he carried it to the nearby schoolhouse where teacher, Anna Young, identified it as belonging to 10-year-old Geneva Hardman. Geneva hadn't arrived for class that day, so the teacher sent two older boys to her house to ensure that she was okay. There, Geneva's mother told them that Geneva had left for school at 7:30, as usual. The anxious woman then joined the students in a search for the missing girl.

That search would soon be joined by several men from the area, and they almost immediately picked up the footprints of a large man and a child, tracking together through the mud. Following those tracks brought them to a tragic scene. Geneva's body was found partly concealed by cattle fodder which had been pulled down over it. A large bloodstained rock lay nearby, and blood had also oozed from a horrific head wound and seeped into the child's clothing. One of the men ran immediately to fetch the Sheriff.

Now a second hunt was launched, this one involving several deputies equipped with bloodhounds. The hounds soon picked up a scent, leading the searchers towards Brannon Crossing. Along that route, they encountered a number of witnesses who reported seeing a local man named Will Lockett, heading north "in a hurry." Lockett was well-known to local law enforcement. He was a black military veteran who these days made his living by bootlegging and through petty theft and housebreaking. The police knew also that there were now several mobs out looking for him and that they were likely to lynch him if they found him first.

Fortunately for Lockett, it was the Sheriff's posse that ran him to ground, taking him into custody near Dixontown just after 4:30 pm that afternoon. From there, he was transported to Lexington and turned over to the Lexington City Police. A dirty and blood-spattered pair of overalls that he'd been carrying at the time of his arrest was confiscated as evidence.

Shortly after his arrival at the police station, Lockett was questioned by Assistant Police Chief Ernest Thompson. During that interview, he confessed to killing Geneva Hardman, saying that he had snatched her as she crossed the field, carried her to a barn and there tried to rape her. He hadn't succeeded because Geneva had put up such a fight. He'd then struck her on the head with a rock, killing her. Asked why he'd committed the murder, he replied simply: "I don't know."

From the moment that he confessed to the crime, Will Lockett was doomed. For a black man murdering a white child in the 1920s, there could be only one outcome. Lockett was going to swing. But the good citizens of Lexington appeared unwilling to allow justice to take its course. Already there were rumors that a mob was gathering. Fearing a lynching, Assistant Chief Thompson ordered Lockett taken to the County Jail. From there, he was taken to the State Reformatory at Frankfort. When even that sturdy building was deemed vulnerable, he was moved to Louisville for his own safety.

The fact that Lockett didn't end up in the hands of a lynch mob can be put down to the foresight of the lawmen involved. At each of the locations where the prisoner had been held, huge crowds started gathering, sometimes missing his departure by mere minutes. The mobs only dispersed once their representatives were allowed to search the premises to confirm that Lockett wasn't there.

There was no hiding, though, when Lockett arrived in Lexington for his trial. By then news of the horrific murder had spread throughout the nation, and troublemakers from across the state had streamed into town, intent on a lynching. Had the governor not called out the Kentucky National Guard, they might well have succeeded.

Inside the courtroom, meanwhile, the trial followed its predictable course. Since Lockett had pleaded guilty, no witnesses were called, and the entire business was concluded within 35 minutes. During that interlude, gunshots were heard frequently from outside as the mob tried to force its way into the building. Six civilians were killed in skirmishes and twenty wounded. Two soldiers were also injured in the fracas, but the line held long enough for the jury to find Lockett guilty and sentence him to death.

William Lockett was put to death in the electric chair at Eddyville State Prison on March 11, 1920. Three days before that execution, he asked to speak to the warden, insisting that he wanted to "come clean." Before several witnesses, he confessed that he'd raped and killed three women, one black and two white. One of these was later identified as Sally Kraft whose decomposed remains had been found in Camp Taylor, a Louisville neighborhood. The other two victims remain unidentified.

Rocky Barton

Rocky Barton had done this before. On that occasion, his attempt to repay a perceived slight with murder had failed. His wife had been clubbed with a shotgun, stabbed three times, and slashed across the throat. Left for dead, she'd survived to testify against her husband at his trial. He had ended up in jail in Kentucky and, unsurprisingly, divorced.

But despite his propensity for violence, his lengthy police record for burglary, for drugs offenses, for DUI, and for assault, Barton appears to have held a fascination for certain women. One of those was Kimbirli Jo Reynolds, who married Barton on June 23, 2001, while he was serving time for the attempted murder of his former wife.

After Barton's release, the couple took up residence in a farmhouse owned by Barton's father just outside of Waynesville, Ohio. But life with Rocky was not easy, as Kimbirli was soon to discover. Her husband was possessive, manipulative, prone to moodiness, and not in the least bit reluctant to use his fists to assure that his version of matrimonial hegemony was maintained. And Kimbirli was no one's idea of a shrinking violet, either. She gave as good as she got and seldom backed down. Her daughter, Tiffany, described the relationship as, "Sometimes good, sometimes bad, the highs were very high, the lows were really low."

But by January 2003, Kimbirli had taken about as much strife as she was going to take. She advised Rocky that she was leaving him and moved out. Then followed a couple of days during which Rocky tried persuading and cajoling her to return before resorting to his old standby of issuing threats. On January 16, he phoned Kimbirli numerous times, shouting and threatening violence. He also made several calls to friends, family and co-workers that day, complaining that Kim had left him and speaking about being sent back to prison and about "his demise." The words should have been a warning to those who heard them.

At around 3:00 p.m. that afternoon, Barton again called Kimbirli. By now, he appeared to have calmed somewhat, so when he asked Kim to come over to the house to pick up her things, she agreed, bringing her 17-year-old daughter, Jamie, with her. They arrived to find Barton's uncle, Larry, waiting outside. Barton then opened the gate, allowing the three of them to drive onto the property while he retreated into the garage. Kimberli had just stepped out of her vehicle when he suddenly emerged from a side door carrying a shotgun.

"You ain't going anywhere, bitch," he screamed at Kimbirli. He was just four feet away when he lifted the shotgun and fired, hitting her in the side. Then, as she collapsed into her daughter's arms, he fired again, this time hitting her in the back from just a foot away.

"I told you I was insane," he said to his Uncle Larry. Then he dropped to his knees, positioned the shotgun barrel under his chin and pulled the trigger.

Two people would be rushed by ambulance from the Waynesville property that day, but only one of them would survive. Kimbirli Barton was D.O.A., having suffered wounds that had shredded her lungs, heart, and liver. Rocky had suffered serious but non-life-threatening injuries to his chin, mouth, and nose. He would require four surgeries to insert pins, wires and screws to hold his jaw together and to keep his eyes from popping out of their sockets. Nonetheless, he would eventually recover sufficiently from his injuries to have his day in court. When that day came around, he made no pretense at innocence and asked for the death penalty. The judge and jury were happy to oblige.

Rocky Barton was put to death by lethal injection on July 12, 2006, less than four years from the day on which he'd taken his wife's life. "I'm sorry for what I done," he said in his last words. "I'm sorry for killing your mama. I'm not asking you to forgive me. Not a day goes by that I'm not trying to forgive myself." He then referenced another condemned man, executed in Utah three decades earlier: "As Gary Gilmore said, 'Let's do it.'"

Alton Coleman

Born in Waukegan, Illinois, on November 6, 1955, Alton Coleman showed signs of abnormal behavior early in life. As a child, he developed the unfortunate habit of wetting his pants, earning him the taunts of his playmates and the nickname "Pissy." That served to distance him from his peers, and he filled in for the lack of interaction by committing acts of vandalism and arson. He also developed an uncanny ability to talk himself out of trouble. By his teens, he already had a lengthy arrest record but had avoided jail time on all but one occasion when he did a two-year stint for robbery.

In 1983, Coleman started dating a mildly retarded young woman named Debra Brown. Brown was engaged to another man at the time, but she ditched her fiancé and moved in with Coleman. She soon learned that her new lover had a prodigious sex drive and was constantly on the lookout for new partners, both male and female. But Brown appears to have been extremely tolerant of Coleman's aberrant drives. She stuck by him even when he was charged with raping his 8-year-old niece in July 1983. And she continued to stand by her man when he was indicted for the rape and murder of 9-year-old Vernita Wheat a year later. When

Coleman told her that he planned to go on the run rather than face the music, Brown insisted on going with him.

On May 31, 1984, Coleman borrowed a car from a friend and drove away from Waukegan for good. Five days later, he and Brown resurfaced in Gary, Indiana. Within weeks of their arrival, they committed a truly horrific crime, kidnapping two girls, aged nine and seven, driving them to some woods and there raping and beating them. The nine-year-old survived. Her seven-year-old niece did not.

Coleman and Brown, meanwhile, had moved on to new targets. On June 1, they abducted 25-year-old Donna Williams, stole her car and beat her to death. Williams' vehicle was later found abandoned in Detroit and provided police with their first lead. A forged identity card, bearing the picture of Debra Brown, was found in the glove compartment. By the time Donna Williams' badly decomposed body was found on July 11, that picture, along with that of Brown's accomplice, would be on the front page of every newspaper in the Midwest.

For now, however, the killers remained at large. On June 28, they were in Dearborn Heights, Michigan, where they broke into a house and severely beat an elderly couple before escaping in their car. They showed up next in Toledo, Ohio, where they raped and murdered Virginia Temple and her 9-year-old daughter, Rachelle. The bodies would later be found hidden in a crawlspace under the Temple residence.

That same day, Coleman and Brown entered the home of Frank and Dorothy Duvendack in Toledo, bound the couple, ransacked their home, and then escaped in their car. On July 12, they were in Over-the-Rhine, Ohio, when 15-year-old Tonnie Storey disappeared. Her body was found eight days later, raped and strangled and with a bracelet belonging to Virginia Temple lying on the ground beside her.

By now, police in Illinois, Wisconsin, Indiana, Ohio and Michigan were hunting the killers. The FBI was also involved, placing Alton Coleman on its Ten Most Wanted List. But still, the fugitives escaped capture. They turned up next in Norwood, Ohio, where they invaded the home of Harry and Marlene Waters, tortured them for three hours, and eventually drove off in their red Plymouth Reliant. Harry Waters suffered massive skull fractures in the attack but survived. His wife was beaten to death. The following day, the killers were in Indianapolis where they murdered 75-year-old Eugene Scott, stole his car, and drove to Evanston, Illinois.

But the net was closing. Aware that Coleman had friends in Evanston, the police had set up surveillance in the town. On July 20, the pair was spotted sitting on the bleachers in Mason Park. Despite being armed with a loaded revolver and a hunting knife, Coleman and Brown surrendered without a fight. The hunt was over. Now came the complex business of serving justice to the heartless killers.

That would prove to be a mammoth task. Coleman and Brown had committed felonies across multiple jurisdictions in six states and understandably each of those states wanted a piece of them. Since Ohio had the strongest evidence and also the death penalty, it was decided to try them there.

Coleman and Brown would ultimately be found guilty of two of the four murder charges they faced. They were both sentenced to death, although Brown's sentence was later commuted to life in prison. Coleman kept his date with the executioner on April 26, 2002, when he was put to death by lethal injection. There can be few criminals who have deserved it more.

Daryl Mack

Betty Jane May was a petite woman of 55 who loved music and reading and had a "tender heart for cats." She was polite but quiet, keeping mostly to herself in the Reno, Nevada, boarding house where she lived. Neighbors would often see her riding her bicycle around town. Betty had once been married, but she and her military husband had divorced after their children were grown.

On the evening of October 28, 1988, Betty's neighbor, Steven Floyd, knocked on her door intending to ask her for a loan. There was no answer and since the door was standing slightly ajar, Floyd pushed it open. He soon spotted Betty, kneeling on the floor with her upper body face down on the bed. He then entered, calling her name. Getting no response, he placed a hand on her shoulder. It was then that he realized she was dead. Floyd immediately went to inform the landlord who called the police.

Betty May had been brutally raped, beaten and murdered, her death attributed to manual strangulation. Despite her diminutive size, she had put up a fight, getting skin tissue caught under her fingernails. Those were collected as evidence. So too were semen samples taken from the victim's vagina and also collected from her left foot. But, of course, DNA testing was still in its infancy back then, and so the samples were never sent for analysis. The murder would remain unsolved for over a decade.

Then, in 1999, a cold case detective reviewed the file. Realizing that the semen and tissue samples had never been sent for analysis, he submitted them to the state lab. Soon after, he got the news he'd been hoping for. There was a match – to a man named Daryl Mack.

Mack wasn't difficult to find. He was currently serving time for the 1994 murder of a prostitute named Kim Parks. Mack had been Parks' pimp back in the early nineties. But on April 8, 1994, the two of them had gotten into an argument after Parks had refused to hand over part of her earnings. Mack had then attacked her, beating her into submission and then strangling her with her own brassiere. He'd then taken her money and left.

Arrested soon after, Mack admitted that he and Parks had fought. According to his version of events, he'd back-handed her, drawing blood. Parks had then given him a share of the money and he'd left. The police hadn't believed him and neither had the judge at the subsequent bench trial. Found guilty, Mack had been sentenced to life in prison without parole.

Now, habitual criminal Daryl Mack, a man with over 20 convictions on his police record, found himself charged with another murder. Again he decided to waive his right to a jury trial and to have his case heard by a panel of three judges. In this case, that was probably a mistake. The case was old and the recollections of witnesses had faded. Any defense lawyer worth his salt could have convinced a jury that there was reasonable doubt. But then there was the DNA evidence which spoke louder than any witness testimony ever could. It placed Mack at the scene and pointed the finger of blame firmly at him. Daryl Mack was found guilty of first-degree murder.

During the penalty phase of the trial, there were representations regarding Mack's difficult childhood and pleas for leniency from his brother and 83-year-old mother. Betty Jane May's children also appeared, asking for justice for the mother who had so brutally been taken from them. Finally, there was Mack, denying involvement in the murder and asking that he be allowed to "continue his rehabilitation in prison." The judges declined that request and sentenced him to death.

Daryl Mack would later waive his appeals, insisting that he wanted to die. He was executed by lethal injection on April 26, 2006, going to his death with a broad grin on his face. Asked if he had any final words, Mack said simply: "Allah is great."

Thomas Stevens & Christopher Burger

It was the night of September 4, 1977, and Christopher Burger, a 17-year-old private stationed at Fort Stewart, Georgia, was out drinking at the enlisted men's club with his friend and fellow serviceman, Thomas Stevens. The two had already consumed a considerable amount of alcohol, but still they wanted to go on partying. Problem was, they were out of money, a situation they decided to remedy by robbing a cab driver.

The soldiers were still debating the logistics of their alcohol-fueled plan when Stevens was told that there was a phone call for him. His squad leader, James Botsford, was on the line. Botsford was at Savannah Municipal Airport and asked Stevens to pick him up. Stevens then returned to Burger, and the two of them went to the kitchen and stole two knives. They then placed a call, summoning a D & M cab.

The driver who had the misfortune of picking up the fare was Roger Honeycutt, a Fort Stewart soldier who supplemented his military income by moonlighting as a cabbie. Honeycutt had taken his fellow soldiers just a few short miles when they drew their knives and forced him to pull over. They then robbed him of $20, all the money he had, and ordered him to remove his clothes. Burger then got behind the wheel while Stevens got in the back seat with Honeycutt. There, he forced the terrified young man to perform fellatio on him before raping him anally. He then tied Honeycutt's hands with the microphone cord from the cab's CB radio and shoved him into the trunk.

Stevens and Burger now drove to the airport to pick up Botsford. And they soon confided what they'd done. When the squad leader refused to believe them, Stevens called out "Are you still back there?" and Botsford heard the reply from the trunk, "Yes, sir." He then encouraged Stevens and Burger to let their captive go. By the time they dropped Botsford off at Fort Stewart, they had agreed to do so.

But Stevens and Burger did not free Honeycutt. Instead, they drove to a Mini Mart in Jesup, Georgia, and bought some sandwiches. Then, after they spotted a police car driving behind them, they decided that it was time to get rid of the cab. Burger drove the vehicle to a wooded area and parked it beside a pond. There, the soldiers wiped it down of prints and Stevens removed the CB radio. Finally, with their captive banging on the lid of the trunk and pleading pitifully to be released, Burger got behind the wheel and got the car rolling towards the pond, jumping free just before it entered the water. The automobile was swiftly sucked towards the depths, taking Roger Honeycutt with it. Stevens and Burger then walked back to the Mini Mart and hailed another cab, paying $11 for the ride back to Fort Stewart.

The next day, Burger and Stevens tracked Botsford down and asked whether he had said anything to authorities. Botsford said that he had not but inquired about the driver. Stevens assured him that they had let the man go. It was only days later, when news of the missing cabbie began to surface, that Botsford went to his superiors and reported what he knew.

Hauled in for questioning, the two young soldiers soon confessed to the murder, although Stevens claimed that he'd been unaware until the last moment that Burger planned on driving the cab into the pond. That attempt to lessen his responsibility helped him not at all. Both men were charged with murder, both were convicted, and both were sentenced to die.

Thomas Stevens was put to death by electrocution at Georgia State Prison on June 28, 1993. Christopher Burger followed him to the chair five months later, on December 7.

Barbara Graham

Barbara Graham was born Barbara Elaine Wood in Oakland, California, on June 26, 1923. She grew up to be a pretty girl with above average intelligence, but one who was at odds with authority from an early age. That rebellious streak would eventually see her sent to the Ventura State School for Girls, the same institution where her mother had spent time as a juvenile.

Released from reform school in 1939, Barbara tried to make a fresh start. She enrolled in business school, hoping to gain the skills that would land her an office job. She also started dating a fellow student, Harry Kielhammer. Before long, Barbara was pregnant, and she and Kielhammer decided to marry. But the union did not last, and by 1941, it had ended in divorce. Thereafter, Barbara resorted to prostitution to make ends meet. She became a "seagull," serving sailors from Oakland Naval Supply Depot. She also traveled to bases as far afield as Long Beach and San Diego, racking up arrests for prostitution in these locations.

By 1945, Barbara was 22 years old, shapely and pretty with a head of luxuriant auburn hair. And she used those assets to good effect, gaining employment at one of San Francisco's most exclusive brothels. There, her ravishing looks gained her a dedicated following of regular clients. But Barbara had by now started using drugs, and that ate up a substantial portion of her earnings. She'd also started frequenting illegal gambling dens and hanging out with criminal types. In 1948, she was sentenced to five years (four suspended) after she perjured herself in providing an alibi for one of her newfound friends.

Barbara spent a year behind bars at the California Department of Corrections Women's Prison in Tehachapi. Emerging from that sentence in 1949, she again made an effort to go straight, moving to Reno, Nevada, and then to Tonopah where she started training as a nurse. But all too soon, she became bored with the lifestyle and boarded a bus for Los Angeles where she resumed her career as a prostitute. In 1953, she married a drug-addicted bartender named Henry Graham. It was through Graham that she met a couple of hardened criminals named Jack Santo and Emmett Perkins. Soon she and Perkins were lovers and he'd roped her into his "next big score," the robbery of 64-year-old Mabel Monahan. Allegedly, the old woman kept a large amount of cash at her Burbank home.

On the evening of March 9, 1953, Barbara knocked on Mrs. Monahan's door and asked if she could use the phone, as her car had broken down. As soon as the elderly widow relented and opened the door, Perkins and Santo, along with associates John True and Baxter Shorter, forced their way in. The gang demanded to know where the money was, but Mrs. Monahan insisted that they were mistaken, that she had no hidden cash. During the interrogation, Barbara reportedly became frustrated and pistol-whipped the old lady, cracking her skull. One of the gang members then suffocated her with a pillow.

The crime had been ill-conceived and badly executed. And the robbers had also erred in including John True in their ranks. True was not a career criminal, and he quickly cracked once the police tracked him down. He agreed to become a state witness in exchange for immunity and was particularly scathing in his assessment of Barbara Graham's role in the victim's death. Once details of the pistol-whipping leaked to the media, Barbara had a new nickname. The press called her "Bloody Babs."

Graham took the stand in her own defense at the trial. She protested her innocence but was damned by John True's evidence. Then she further damaged her defense by offering a fellow inmate $25,000 to provide her with an alibi. Unbeknownst to her, the inmate was working with the police.

Graham, Santo, and Perkins were ultimately sentenced to death for the murder of Mabel Monahan. The sentence, of course, went on appeal, but once that was rejected, Barbara was transferred to San Quentin where her execution was scheduled to take place on June 2, 1955.

There was still plenty of drama to come, though. As she was being led to the gas chamber, a call came from the governor, delaying the execution. On hearing the news, Barbara collapsed and had to be carried back to the holding cell. Twenty minutes later, the phone rang again, authorizing the warder to resume. This time, Graham made it all the way into the execution chamber before there was another call and another return to the cells. "I can't take this anymore," the distraught woman sobbed. "Why are they torturing me like this?"

The reason, although Graham didn't know it, was that her attorney was making a last desperate bid to save her life. That bid, ultimately, would fail. Her third walk to the execution chamber would be her last. Barbara Graham's final words were: "Good people are always so sure they're right."

Johnny Ray Johnson

A horrendously brutal rape slayer, Johnny Ray Johnson would eventually be executed for the 1995 murder of Leah Joette Smith. But as savage as that crime was, it was only the tip of a decades-long campaign of sexual violence against women perpetrated by the Houston taxi driver. Johnson was responsible for at least three murders, as well as countless violent rapes and numerous assaults.

Johnson's career of evil can be traced back to 1975, when he was 18 years old and raped his eight-year-old niece, threatening to kill the child if she told anyone. He next appears on the radar in 1983, when he was convicted of sexual assault in Travis County and sentenced to five years in prison. Upon his release, he found employment driving cabs in Houston, the perfect cover for the new ruse he'd developed. He'd lure prostitutes into his vehicle, drive them out to the country and then beat and rape them before driving off with their money and clothes, leaving them naked and miles away from the city.

None of these women ever reported the crimes since they feared police indifference and possible reprisals from Johnson. The brutish cab driver might have gotten away with it indefinitely had he not started preying on his ordinary customers as well. One woman was raped and beaten after she refused Johnson's offer of $20 for sex. She immediately reported the assault to the police, and Johnson found himself back in custody. He would ultimately be sent down for another five-year prison term.

Released in 1991, Johnson married a prostitute named Dora Ann Moseley and moved with her to Austin. But the union ended in 1994 after Johnson inflicted such a vicious beating on his wife that she would probably have died had a neighbor not called 911. That horrific assault earned Johnny Ray Johnson a meager six months in prison. Soon after his release in 1994, he graduated to murder.

According to his confession, Johnson's first victim was a woman he met on 11th Street in Austin. The two spent some time together, drinking and smoking crack, but when he tried to have sex with the woman, she refused, producing a razor and slashing his neck. Johnson fought back, beating his companion into submission before forcing himself on her. He then slashed her throat, watched her bleed to death, and then used the razor to cut off her head. He carried that away with him, using it later for what he described as "irregular sex."

In December 1994, Johnson returned to Houston where he carried out several knifepoint rapes before he committed the murder that would ultimately send him to death row. Leah Smith was a drug-addicted hooker who agreed to have sex with Johnson in exchange for some crack cocaine. However, after smoking the crack, Leah reneged on the deal and refused to sleep with him. Angered by her refusal, Johnson grabbed her by the throat, ripped her clothing and then threw her to the ground. When she fought back, he struck her head repeatedly against the cement curb. He then raped her, after which he stomped on her face five or six times and left her for dead.

Leah Smith's badly decomposed body was found on March 27, 1995, in a water-filled gully near some railroad tracks. An autopsy would later determine that she had suffered severe injuries to her mouth, face, head, and neck. Her teeth were knocked out, and both sides of her jaw were fractured. Death, though, was due to drowning on her own blood as it accumulated in the back of her throat.

One month later, on April 28, the partially clothed body of a woman was found under a highway overpass in Houston. She had sustained massive head injuries, while markings on her throat suggested that her killer had stomped on her. A bloodstained breezeblock was found at the scene, suggesting that it had been used to inflict the head trauma. Johnson would later confirm this in his confession.

Johnny Ray Johnson went on trial in Houston in May 1996. With his confession forming the basis of the prosecution case, there was never any doubt as to the outcome. Found guilty of the first-degree murder of Leah Joette Smith, Johnson was sentenced to death. He was executed by lethal injection on February 12, 2009.

Stephen Morin

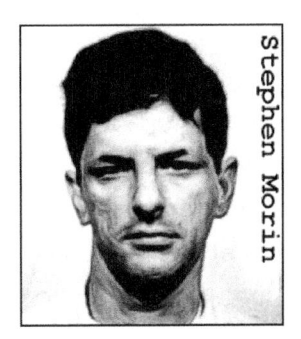

There can't be many death row inmates who refer to their execution as their "Graduation Day." But that was the case with Stephen Peter Morin. Morin, you see, had become a born-again Christian on death row and had decided that if the Lord wanted him to die, then he would submit to His authority. As a result, he waived all appeals and ended up strapped to a gurney at the Huntsville Unit in Texas on March 13, 1985, just four years after he'd been sentenced to death. But how had Morin ended up in this situation in the first place? To answer that question, we have to follow a lifelong journey of rape and murder during which the drug-addicted Morin became a suspect in thirty felonies and ended up on the FBI's Most Wanted list.

Stephen Morin was born on February 19, 1951, in Providence, Rhode Island. We don't know a lot about his background, but we do know that he ended up in Nevada in the early 80s. There, he started taking long drives along the desolate stretches of highway that crisscross that state. And wherever Morin ventured, the bodies of dead and brutalized women seemed to turn up – 15-year-old Kim Bryant, killed by blunt force trauma to the head; Linda Jenkins, beaten, strangled and then dumped in the desert; Susan Belotte, age 18, strangled and dumped.

All of these the victims had been kidnapped from Las Vegas and murdered within the space of a single year between 1980 and 1981. But while the police strongly suspected that a single perpetrator was responsible, it was impossible to prove in those pre-DNA days. Stephen Morin, in any case, did not appear on any suspect list.

Then, the discovery of Cheryl Ann Daniels' body, in an area appropriately named Hell Hole Canyon, finally put Morin in the frame. Cheryl had been raped, beaten and eventually strangled to death. But her killer had made a serious mistake. He'd dropped his wallet at the scene and although it contained no identification, it did contain a note with the name and address of a young woman who turned out to be a co-worker of the victim. Questioned by police, Sara Pisan said that the note had been written by a man named Andrew Generoso who had been pestering her to go out with him. She'd spurned his advances, she said, because she found him "creepy."

The police now had a name for their suspect, even if that name was an alias. Andrew Generoso was actually Stephen Morin. And Morin had, in any case, quit the state. He'd always had a nose for trouble, and after realizing that he'd lost his wallet, he'd decided that it might be time to move on. Over the months that followed, he spent time in California and Colorado before heading eventually to Texas.

In the early morning hours of December 11, 1981, 21-year-old Carrie Marie Scott was leaving her job at Maggie's Restaurant in San Antonio when she found a man trying to hotwire her car in the parking lot. Carrie yelled at the man, but to her surprise, he didn't run off. He continued fiddling under the dashboard and in the next moment the engine roared into life. The man then straightened up and warned Carrie to back off. She, however, was not about to allow her car to be taken without a fight. She angrily approached the car thief. That was a bad mistake. Morin drew a gun and shot her dead where she stood.

But the shooting left Morin with a problem. He knew that the police would now be looking for the vehicle, and so he dumped it at a local shopping center. A short while later, he abducted another young woman, Margaret Palm, from that same center, forced her into her own car and told her to drive.

Here, the story takes a decidedly strange twist. Rather than following his usual M.O., Morin spent all day driving around with Margaret Palm. Later, he instructed her to drop him off at a bus station and then told her that she was free to go. When the police arrived a short while later, they found him reading a handwritten book of Bible verses which his captive had given him. He surrendered without a fight. Later, he'd credit Margaret Palm with converting him to Christianity.

At the time of his arrest, Morin was a suspect of at least thirty murders with some law enforcement officials putting the number as high as 44. However, he was tried and convicted of just one – Carrie Marie Scott. Later, on death row, he'd admit to murdering Janna Bruce in Corpus Christi, Texas, and Shelia Whalen in Golden, Colorado. As for the other murders, Morin insisted that "Christ has wiped them from my memory."

Stephen Morin was executed by lethal injection on March 13th, 1985.

William Wesley Chappell

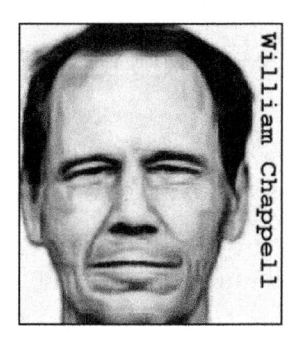

"This isn't over yet. I'll get you for this."

Those were the chilling words spoken by William Wesley Chappell to his former girlfriend's family as he was being led away to begin a prison term for indecent assault. That charge had arisen out of a bizarre set of circumstances. In 1981, 44-year-old Chappell had started dating a 15-year-old girl named Jane Sitton who, despite her tender years, already had a child. Jane's family had frowned on the relationship, but despite their disapproval, it endured for over two years until 1983. During that time, Chappell would regularly be seen attending football games with Jane at her school. He even escorted her to her prom.

It was only after the relationship soured that allegations of child molestation began to surface. Chappell was accused of indecently assaulting Jane's three-year-old daughter, an accusation that would eventually see him brought to trial. There, the evidence given by Jane and by her grandmother, 49-year-old Martha

Lindsey, saw him convicted and sentenced to five years in prison. Chappell immediately lodged an appeal and was released on bond pending those proceedings. It was then that he began plotting his revenge.

Chappell's original plan was to burn down the Lindsey residence with all of the family members inside. In fact, he made an attempt to do just that, recruiting his wife, Sally Hayes, to drive him to the home in Fort Worth, Texas. However, the fire did not take hold and although it caused damage to the family's kitchen, no one was hurt. Chappell was reportedly furious when he heard the news.

Not that it deflected him from his vengeful path. On May 3, 1988, he decided to try again, this time using a more reliable method. At around 10:30 a.m. on that day, Chappell and Hayes left their Tennessee home and drove west towards Texas, arriving in Fort Worth at around 8:30 that evening. Chappell then told Hayes to take the wheel while he got into the back and changed into dark clothing and a wig. He also had a nylon tote bag containing a walkie-talkie, a 9-mm pistol, gloves, a ski-mask, and burglary tools.

By 9:00 p.m., they were cruising the Lindseys' neighborhood, and Chappell then instructed Hayes to let him out and to drive around until he called her on the walkie-talkie. That call came some 20 minutes later, and Hayes then picked her husband up. He was in an obviously excited state, telling her that he'd shot Jane, Martha Lindsay, and Martha's husband, 71-year-old Elbert Sitton. The pair then drove back to Tennessee.

But Chappell was mistaken, both in the identity of his victims and in the condition he'd left them in. It wasn't Jane that he'd executed, but her half-sister, Alexandra Heath, who'd been shot to death as she lay asleep in her bed. And neither Martha nor Elbert Sitton was dead. Martha would die in hospital two days later without ever regaining consciousness; Elbert would survive for two months before he succumbed to his wounds. During that time, he told the police that although the intruder had worn a mask, he was certain that it was William Chappell who'd shot him and his family.

Chappell would eventually be charged with capital murder and extradited back to Texas to stand trial. He denied any involvement in the shootings but, unfortunately for him, the prosecutor had struck a deal with Sally Hayes, and once she gave her testimony, there could be only one outcome.

William Chappell was found guilty and sentenced to death in November 1989. He would spend the next 13 years going through the appeals process before time eventually ran out for him on November 20, 2002. His final words were directed at Jane Sitton, insisting that he'd never molested her daughter and denying that he'd killed her family.

William Hance

Between September 1977 and April 1978, the city of Columbus, Georgia, was plagued by a series of six horrendous rape-murders. The killer would ultimately be identified as Carlton Gary, a black serial killer who preyed on elderly white women and went by the nickname "The Stocking Strangler." So outraged were Georgians by these crimes that another, particularly savage, slaying went almost unnoticed.

On September 6, 1977, the nude body of 24-year-old army private, Karen Hickman, was found near the women's barracks at Fort Benning. She'd been beaten to death with a blunt instrument, then apparently run over several times with a motor vehicle. Forensics suggested that the murder had occurred elsewhere, and that the killer had subsequently transported the body to an area where it was certain to be discovered. Clues, however, were few and far between, and the case initially went unsolved.

A month after the murder, the police received an anonymous phone call directing them to an area where Hickman's clothes could be found. Investigators had since learned that the victim had lived a promiscuous lifestyle and had favored picking up black soldiers in bars. Her death, they decided, was more than likely the result of a date gone bad, an isolated crime that was unlikely to be repeated. They'd soon be proven wrong on that score.

On March 3, 1978, the Columbus chief of police received a letter, purportedly from a white supremacist group called the "Forces of Evil." It demanded the capture of the Stocking Strangler, threatening violence if this did not happen. "Since that coroner said the Strangler is black," the note read, "we decided to come here and try to catch him or put more pressure on you. From now on black women in Columbus, Georgia, will be disappearing if the Strangler is not caught."

The letter went on to state that a local black woman named Gail Jackson had already been abducted and that she would be killed if the Stocking Strangler was not caught by June 1. Two more blacks would be killed if the murderer was still at large on September 1.

Senior police officers who examined the letter were convinced that it was a hoax. And this observation appeared to be validated when a search of police records turned up no one named Gail Jackson who had been reported missing in Columbus. As their investigation continued, however, it found that a black prostitute, Brenda Gail Faison, had disappeared from a local tavern on February 28. Could this be the hostage that the letter was referring to? While detectives were still mulling that possibility, a second letter arrived on March 13. The writer now suggested that a ransom of $10,000 might secure the hostage's release.

Two weeks later, a third note arrived, claiming that another hostage, named Irene, had been abducted and was scheduled to die on June 1 if the Stocking Strangler case was not resolved. This note was written on military stationary, leading detectives to speculate that the writer might be a soldier stationed at Fort Benning. And they soon had a lead on the woman referenced in the letter. Thirty-two-year-old Irene Thirkield had disappeared on March 16 after being seen in the company of an unnamed black soldier. A search was launched but no trace was found of the missing woman.

In the early hours of March 30, 1978, an anonymous caller directed MPs to a shallow grave just outside the military base. In it, they found the remains of Brenda Faison, her skull shattered and her face beaten to a bloody pulp. Four days later, another call, this time to the police, led to Irene Thirkield's headless corpse hidden behind a pile of logs on the army base.

On April 4, military police asked a number of Fort Benning officers to review tape recordings of the anonymous phone calls in the hope that one of them might recognize the caller's voice. It was a long shot, but it paid off. One of the officers thought that it sounded like a soldier under his command, 26-year-old Private William Hance.

Hance was arrested that same day, and soon after confessed to the murders of Brenda Faison, Irene Thirkield, and Karen Hickman. He later recanted his confessions, but a civilian jury found him guilty anyway. He was sentenced to death and died in Georgia's electric chair on March 31, 1994.

Elmo Lee Smith

On the morning of December 18, 1959, 17-year-old Joyce Ann Davis was walking near her home in Roxborough, Pennsylvania, when she was accosted by a scrawny man driving a white-and-brown Chevy Bel Air. The man tried to drag her into his vehicle. When she resisted, he drew a knife and stabbed her five times before speeding off, leaving her sprawled on the sidewalk. She'd later receive stitches to her injuries and remain hospitalized for five days.

In the days that followed, police in nearby Bridgeport received several reports of a prowler, sneaking through alleyways and attempting to break into houses. Then, two days after Christmas, a man matching the general description surfaced in Phoenixville where he tried to snatch three 12-year-old girls from a sidewalk and force them into his two-tone Bel Air.

By now, Montgomery County police were becoming increasingly concerned. Their jurisdiction was generally a peaceful place where violent crime was all but unheard of. Yet here was this gaunt stranger, prowling the streets and clearly intent on doing somebody harm. How long before he succeeded? The answer to that question was not long in coming.

On the evening of Monday, December 29, 16-year-old Maryann Mitchell boarded a bus near her home in Manayunk. Maryann was a quiet, diligent girl who attended Cecelian Academy and had ambitions of becoming a nurse. That evening, she was headed for the Roxy theater in Roxborough. There, she hooked up with two school friends, and they attended an evening performance of South Pacific. After the show, they stopped off at a diner for burgers before parting company at around 10:30. Maryann then headed to a nearby bus stop to get her ride home. The distance (later measured by detectives) was 112 steps. Maryann didn't make it.

Maryann Mitchell had never missed a curfew in her life. So when she failed to arrive home by 11 o'clock, her parents were immediately concerned. At around 11:30, they called the police and, within hours, a search had been launched for the missing teenager. It would resolve itself tragically 28 hours later.

At around 2 p.m. on December 30, 1959, four highway department employees were driving along a desolate strip of blacktop called Hart's Lane when they spotted what looked like a mannequin lying in a gully. Closer inspection proved them wrong. It was not a mannequin but the semi-naked body of a young girl, savagely beaten to death. The men ran immediately to call the police. It did not take long to identify the victim. Maryann Mitchell was still wearing the class ring bearing her initials.

An autopsy report would later reveal that Maryann had been repeatedly raped before being beaten to death with a heavy object that had fractured her skull in several places. The medical examiner also concluded that she'd been dead only 12 hours, suggesting that her killer had kept her alive for an extended period before he decided to end her life. That suggested to police that he was not a first-timer. He'd done this before.

In any investigation of this type, one of the most obvious courses of action is to question known sex offenders living in the area. That was what detectives now started doing, a line of inquiry that led them to a man named Elmo Lee Smith. Smith was a habitual criminal who'd only recently been paroled from a 10-year prison term for rape. He was also a suspect in several murders. Smith remained cool under questioning but was unable to account for the scratches on his face, which had quite obviously been made by human fingernails. It was therefore decided to take him into custody.

In the meantime, a search warrant had been obtained for Smith's apartment. It turned up blood-spattered clothes and shoes. Then an even bigger clue emerged. Inside the stolen Chevy Bel Air that Smith had been driving, detectives found a prayer book that belonged to Maryann Mitchell. They also uncovered the probable murder weapon, a bumper jack matted with dried blood and hair.

The evidence was rapidly stacking up against Smith, but still he denied involvement in Maryann's murder. It was only when detectives pressed him to take a polygraph that he eventually cracked and admitted that he'd killed her. He'd later retract that confession, but it would do him no good.

Elmo Lee Smith was brought to trial for the murder of Maryann Mitchell in August 1960, with the proceedings moved to Gettysburg because of the extreme hostility towards him in Montgomery County. His eventual conviction on September 1, 1960, saw him greeted by a 500-strong crowd chanting "Hang him! Hang him!" as he was led to a waiting vehicle.

Smith, of course, would not be hanged. His well-deserved oblivion was delivered via the electric chair on April 2, 1962. He was the last man put to death in Pennsylvania's version of 'Old Sparky.'

Reginald Perkins

Reginald Perkins was a consummate liar, an arch manipulator, and the brutal slayer of at least six women over a 28-year period. Add to that innumerable rapes, countless robberies, and a plethora of other felonies, and you have what amounts to a one-man crime spree. Still, according to Perkins, he never did anything wrong. Even as the needle was being inserted into his arm on the day of his execution, he continued to claim that the state of Texas was "murdering" an innocent man.

Born in Arkansas on April 29, 1955, Perkins was raised in Texas, and later relocated to Cleveland, Ohio. By 1979, he was working as a truck driver in that city when he met Ramola Washington. The couple started dating, and a year later Washington moved out of her sister's home to live with Perkins.

Shortly after these new living arrangements were in effect, Washington asked Perkins to return a set of house keys to her sister, Paulette Nelson. Three days later, having heard nothing from Paulette, Washington went to her house on Sowinski Avenue. She found Paulette, 21, lying on the bed, her face mottled and her throat bearing the signs of strangulation. Her infant daughter lay in bed beside her, malnourished and dehydrated but otherwise unharmed. Although Romala Washington didn't know it at the time, it was her live-in lover who had done the vile deed.

And Paulette Nelson wasn't the only one to meet a violent death at Perkins' hands during that period. While Perkins was living with Ramola Washington, he fathered a child by another young woman, Thelma Morman. Thelma's mother, Jennie, lived in an apartment on East 93rd Street. On a Sunday evening in January 1981, Jennie's family phoned the apartment after she failed to show up for a family card game. When she didn't answer, they became worried and went to check on her. They found Jennie dead in the bedroom with two pillows over her face, a scarf knotted tightly around her neck.

Perkins, meanwhile, was living on East 79th Street, just a few blocks away. On December 11, 1981, he lured 12-year-old Lashelle Thomas into a vacant house where he beat the girl and tried to rape her. But Lashelle fought so hard and screamed so loudly that a friend came to her rescue, and Perkins was forced to let her go. He warned Lashelle that he'd kill her if she told anyone about the attack.

Terrified by his threats, Lashelle said nothing. However, the friend told Lashelle's mother, Jerry Dean Thomas, and she confronted Perkins. A few days later, Lashelle arrived home from school to find her mother sitting in a chair, the cord of a hairdryer pulled tightly around her neck.

Perkins was immediately suspected, and although the police were certain that he'd strangled all three women, they lacked the evidence to prove it. They did, however, have him on the attempted rape and assault of Lashelle Thomas, and a conviction in that case earned him six to 25 years.

Perkins was back on the streets in 1987 and, shortly thereafter, returned to Texas to live with his father and stepmother. On May 6, 1991, Shirley Douglas, 44, and her aunt Hattie Wilson, 79, were strangled to death in their home. Perkins had been dating Wilson's granddaughter. Two years later, Perkins was arrested on a parole violation and shipped back to Ohio to complete his sentence. He was released in 1996 and once again returned to Texas where his stepmother, Gertie Mae Perkins, hired him as a truck driver in the family business. She also gave him a mobile home.

On December 4, 2000, ten months after setting her stepson up with a job and a home, Gertie Mae Perkins vanished. That same day, Perkins used his driver's license to pawn her wedding ring and soon found himself under arrest. Under interrogation, he quickly cracked and led police to a parking garage where Gertie's body was found in the trunk of her car. She'd been beaten and strangled to death.

Perkins was convicted of murder and sentenced to die, a sentence that was carried out by lethal injection on January 22, 2009. He has since been linked by DNA evidence to the murders of Paula Nelson, Jennie Morman, Jerry Thomas, Hattie Wilson, and Shirley Douglas.

Dalton Prejean

Dalton Prejean was born on December 10, 1959, in Lafayette, Louisiana, the second of four children. When he was just two weeks old, he was sent to live with an aunt and uncle in Houston, Texas, and he grew up believing that they were his biological parents. It was only when his father moved to Houston in the early seventies that he learned the truth.

The revelation about his parentage seemed to have a profound effect on Dalton. He started skipping school and acting out, becoming such a problem that he was eventually sent back to Lafayette to live with his mother. That hardly helped the situation. In 1972, after a series of juvenile misdemeanors, he ended up at the Louisiana Training Institute. Released seven months later, he graduated to more serious crimes, including burglary and arson. That landed him a stint at the Lafayette Juvenile Youth Authority, although he escaped within a month and never returned.

In June of 1974, 14-year-old Dalton Prejean and two friends decided to rob a cab driver. Armed with a .22 revolver, the youths flagged down a taxi driven by John Doucet and directed the driver to a quiet street. There, they asked him to stop while they searched for an address. At this point, the boy who had the gun was supposed to draw it and threaten the driver. But the youth appeared nervous, and so Prejean grabbed the weapon from him. Almost immediately, he fired, hitting Doucet in the head and killing him. The three boys then fled, although Prejean handed himself over to the police later that evening. He admitted the killing but claimed that he had thought the driver was going for a gun.

Subjected to psychiatric evaluation in the wake of the shooting, Prejean was diagnosed with borderline mental retardation. Because of his age, he was sent back to the Lafayette Juvenile Youth Authority with the recommendation that he should be held until age twenty. But that ruling was overturned after a second assessment in 1976. Prejean walked free on December 10 of that year, released into the custody of his aunt with no probation requirements. Within seven months, he would kill again.

On the night of July 1, 1977, Prejean was out partying in Lafayette with his brother, Joseph, and friends Michael George and Michael Broussard. The foursome had visited several bars in the area and ended up at Roger's Nite Club where they drank into the morning hours of July 2, eventually leaving at around 5 a.m.

They were driving a 1966 Chevy with Prejean at the wheel and his brother beside him in the passenger seat. However, the car had a broken taillight and they had traveled only a few hundred feet from the club when they were pulled over by Louisiana State Trooper George Cleveland.

Prejean brought the car to a stop, but since he did not have a driver's license, he attempted to switch places with his brother. This was noticed by Cleveland who first ordered all of the occupants out of the vehicle, then told Prejean, George and Broussard to get back in. The officer then started searching Joseph Prejean, but Dalton took exception to the way the trooper pushed his brother against the car. "I don't like the way he's doing my brother," he told his companions. Then he reached under the seat and removed the .38-caliber revolver he kept hidden there.

Trooper Cleveland never saw him coming. He was still patting Joseph down when Dalton Prejean rounded the vehicle, lifted the gun and fired twice without warning. The Prejean brothers then jumped back into the car and sped away, leaving the officer dead in the street. Unbeknownst to them, someone had witnessed the shooting and noted their license plate number. Within hours, all four men were in custody. And it was soon clear who had fired the fatal shots.

Dalton Prejean was charged with first-degree murder and brought to trial in Ouachita Parish, Louisiana on May 1, 1978. Just three days later, the proceedings were concluded with Prejean found guilty and sentenced to death. Despite objections over his youth and mental capacity, he was put to death in the electric chair at Louisiana State Penitentiary on May 18, 1990.

Ellis Wayne Felker

An argument often raised by capital punishment opponents is that there is always a possibility that an innocent man will be convicted and put to death. This is a valid concern, as the infamous cases of Ruben Cantu, Larry Griffin, and Carlos de Luna illustrate. In each of these instances, there is significant evidence to suggest that the wrong man was executed. The case of Ellis Wayne Felker, though often mentioned in the same context, is somewhat more ambiguous.

On the morning of December 8, 1981, a vagrant was hunting for soda bottles along Scuffle Creek in Twiggs County, Georgia, when he spotted something in the water. That turned out to be the body of 19-year-old student Evelyn Joy Ludlam, missing for two weeks. Although fully clothed when she was discovered, an autopsy would reveal that Joy Ludlam had been raped and sodomized. She had then been strangled and had been dead by the time she was placed in the water.

Police inquiries soon led detectives to the Holiday Inn in Warner Robins, where Joy had worked as a cocktail waitress. There, they learned of an interaction she'd had with a customer on Monday, November 23, 1981, the evening before she went missing. According to her colleagues, Joy had struck up a conversation with a young man, wearing a t-shirt advertising "The Leather Shoppe." Looking into the business, investigators found that it was owned by an ex-con named Ellis Wayne Felker who had only been released that April. Felker had served five years of an eight-year sentence for kidnapping and forcibly sodomizing a young woman in 1976. This, of course, made him a strong suspect in the Ludlam murder.

And that belief was strengthened when detectives spoke to Felker's neighbors. One of them revealed that she'd been asked by Felker's mother to write down the license plate number of every vehicle that visited the property. Going over that list, detectives picked up that Joy's car had been parked outside Felker's house from 9:00 a.m. to 11:00 a.m. on November 24, the day after Joy's chance meeting with Felker. The car would later turn up abandoned in a parking lot.

Felker was now brought in for questioning. Under interrogation, he admitted meeting with Joy at the Holiday Inn and at his house. However, he offered an innocent explanation. He said that Joy had been unhappy working at the Holiday Inn and had been looking for a new job. He'd suggested that she might be interested in running his leather business and had met with her the next day to show her his shop. With no way to prove otherwise, the police were forced to let him go. However, Felker was still considered the main suspect and remained under constant police surveillance.

Between December 1981 and March 1982, Felker's house and car were searched several times with the police discovering hair and fibers that linked him to Joy Ludlam. Since Felker did not deny interacting with Joy, most of those could be easily explained away. What was more difficult to explain was the presence of his head and beard hair on the victim's underclothes and the presence of the victim's pubic hair in Felker's house. On March 29, 1982, Ellis Wayne Felker was arrested and charged with murder.

Felker would ultimately be tried, convicted and sentenced to death for Joy Ludlam's murder. He would die in the electric chair at the State Prison in Jackson, Georgia, on November 15, 1996.

So why the controversy over what appears to be a fairly clear-cut case? Much of it centers on time of death. The original autopsy report stated that Joy had been dead for five days when she was found. This suggests that she must have been kept alive for over a week. Since Felker was under police surveillance at the time, he could not have been the killer. Later, the autopsy report would be amended to the more open ended "at least five days." Was this done to accommodate Felker as a suspect?

It was also revealed that prosecutors at Felker's trial withheld boxes of evidence, including DNA samples, which might have exonerated Felker. When that material was eventually tested (after Felker's death) the results were inconclusive. Additionally, there was another suspect, a man who had confessed to the crime.

The confession was dismissed because the suspect was considered to be "mentally retarded."

The issue of Ellis Wayne Felker's guilt or innocence remains unresolved, but the question of innocence before the law does not. Under the principle of reasonable doubt, Felker should probably have been acquitted.

Carl Hall & Bonnie Heady

On the morning of September 28, 1953, someone rang the doorbell at the exclusive French Institute of Notre Dame school in Kansas City, Missouri. When Sister Morand answered it, she found a plump, middle-aged woman standing there, sobbing despairingly. She said that she was the aunt of Bobby Greenlease, a first-grader at the school. Bobby's mother had suffered a heart attack and was in St. Mary's Hospital. She was asking for her son.

Sister Morand asked the woman to wait in the chapel. Then she rushed down the corridor and returned minutes later with a cherub-faced, blond boy. She found the woman on her knees in one of the pews, praying sobbingly for her sister's recovery. This show of devotion convinced the nun that the woman was who she claimed to be. Moments later, Bobby's "aunt" was leading him down the steps to a waiting cab.

Unfortunately, Sister Morand's trust had been misplaced. The woman who had taken Bobby Greenlease wasn't his aunt; she was a low-life grifter named Bonnie Heady. Now, Heady directed the cab driver to the intersection of Main and 40th Streets where she got out and led the boy across the street to a waiting Plymouth station wagon. There was a man sitting in the driver's seat. Checking his wing mirror, he guided the Plymouth from the curb and into traffic, headed south.

The man behind the wheel of the Plymouth was Carl Austin Hall, a once-pampered rich kid who'd resorted to a life of crime after squandering his $200,000 inheritance. Up until the Greenlease kidnapping, Hall had been strictly small time. His usual gig was holding up cab drivers at gunpoint, an enterprise that had earned him a five-year stint in the Missouri State Prison. Hall had been paroled in April 1953, after serving 16 months of that term. Just five months later and he and his partner Heady had hit the big time. They'd snatched Robert Greenlease Jr., son of one of the wealthiest men in Kansas City.

The day after the kidnapping, Robert Greenlease Sr. received a ransom note, demanding $600,000 in exchange for Bobby's life. Greenlease immediately contacted his bank to make arrangements for the withdrawal of the funds. But the kidnappers took their time following up after their initial contact. They seemed in no hurry to conclude the transaction. Greenlease was left with the distinct impression that they were taunting him. In fact, unbeknownst to Greenlease, his son was already dead.

Hall had never had any intention of holding Bobby for ransom. After picking up Heady and the boy in downtown Kansas City, he'd driven to an abandoned farm in Johnson County. There he'd tried to strangle Bobby. When that failed, he drew his gun and shot the six-year-old in the chest before pumping two more bullets into his brain. He and Heady then drove back to their home in St. Joseph, Missouri, where they dropped the tiny corpse into a shallow grave in the garden.

On October 4, 1953, Robert Greenlease Sr. ordered the police and FBI to stand down and arranged for a driver to drop a duffel bag containing $600,000 in cash along a stretch of Highway 40. This was the area designated by Hall, and he phoned the Greenlease home later that evening to confirm that he'd made the pickup. He promised that Bobby would be released as soon as he'd had a chance to count the money.

That, of course, was never going to happen. While the frantic parents waited for news of their beloved boy, Hall and Heady were heading for St. Louis. There they hit the town, spending lavishly and getting falling down drunk. They then checked into a hotel room where Heady passed out and Hall seized the opportunity to skip out on his partner.

But Carl Hall had never been the smartest of criminals. Rather than getting out of town, he simply moved to another hotel where he flashed money around with such abandon that a hotel employee decided it was best to inform the police. Hall was arrested in his hotel room, still nursing a hangover. He promptly gave up Bonnie Heady, and it wasn't long before they'd both admitted to killing Bobby Greenlease. Later, they'd try to withdraw their confessions but, by then, it was too late. Found guilty of murder, Hall and Heady were sentenced to death.

Carl Hall and Bonnie Heady went to the gas chamber together on December 18, 1953. "Thanks for everything," Heady told the warder before the chamber was sealed. She then turned to Hall. "Are you all right, honey?" she asked. "Yes, Momma," he replied in a quivering voice. Moments later the cyanide pellets were released.

Leo Edwards Jr.

Leo Edwards was a self-proclaimed "bad man," a lifelong criminal who had been in and out of prison since his teens. During that time, he'd racked up convictions for burglary, for theft, and for armed robbery. His latest burglary conviction, in 1978, had seen him sentenced to a six-year term at the Louisiana State Prison. Edwards, however, did not intend to serve out that time. He immediately began plotting his escape, recruiting a fellow inmate named Mikel Leroy White to his cause. In June 1980, the pair managed to pull off their escape, fleeing across the state border to Mississippi. What followed would be a five-day orgy of violence which would leave three innocent people ruthlessly gunned down.

Edwards and White were already four days into their rampage by the time they arrived in Jackson, Mississippi, on June 14. Already, two people, a bar owner and a store clerk, had been shot to death in holdups. This time, they had their eye on a convenience store where Lindsey Don Dixon was on duty behind the counter. Dixon offered no resistance when Edwards pointed a gun at him and demanded the contents of the register. To do so would have been foolish. He handed over the $111 in crumpled bills that lay in the cash tray without hesitation. Edwards nonetheless pulled the trigger, shooting the clerk in the face and killing him instantly.

Had the fugitives left town immediately, fled the jurisdiction and gotten rid of the murder weapon, it would have been unlikely that the murder would ever have been pinned on them. But the pair foolishly hung around, and Edwards made matters worse by getting into an argument with a woman the next day, during which he drew a gun and threatened to shoot her. The police were called, catching Edwards and White at the scene and confiscating Edwards' handgun. Test fired, it produced a ballistic match to the weapon that had killed Lindsey Dixon.

Edwards, as he was prone to do in these circumstances, hung tough, challenging the police to prove that it was he who had fired the fatal shot. Unfortunately for him, his partner-in-crime proved to be far more pliable. Facing the prospect of the death penalty, Mikel White cracked and asked for a deal – his testimony against Edwards in exchange for life in prison.

Leo Edwards would eventually be convicted in Mississippi and sentenced to death. But that sentence was far from the end of the matter. Over the next nine years, he would drag the matter through various appellate courts. His main contention was that of racial bias. He was a black man convicted by an all-white jury, and he felt that he had been unfairly treated.

Unfortunately for Edwards, the courts did not share his views, and neither did Mississippi governor, Ray Mabus. "Leo Edwards is a mass murderer who killed in cold blood," Mabus stated in response to Edwards' clemency petition. "He tried and failed to get relief in sixteen appeals to the courts. Discrimination had no bearing on his case. Edwards' sentence is a result of his own crime."

And with that, Leo Edwards' fate was sealed. Just after midnight on June 21, 1989, he was led to the gas chamber at the State Penitentiary in Parchman, Mississippi. He was strapped into the chair and the chamber was sealed. Cyanide pills were then dropped into a bucket of sulphuric acid, stirring up a fog of lethal gas. Edwards at first appeared to be holding his breath, but then he gasped suddenly and slumped forward. He was pronounced dead at 12:15 a.m.

Kevin Conner

There can be few killers in Indiana's history who have acted with such wanton savagery as 23-year-old Kevin Conner. On the evening of January 26, 1988, Conner was hanging out and drinking with friends Tony Moore, 24, Steven Wentland, 19, and Bruce Voge, 19, at Moore's residence in Indianapolis. At some point during the evening, Moore, Wentland, and Conner decided to go for a drive, while Voge stayed behind at the house. Since they were in Wentland's car, he slid behind the wheel while Moore got into the passenger seat and Conner got into the back. They'd not traveled far when an argument broke out between Wentland and Moore.

The reason for the altercation is not known, but it became more and more heated by the minute. It terminated when Moore accepted a knife handed to him by Conner and plunged it into Wentland's side. That caused Wentland to slam on the brakes. Before the car had even come to its swerving halt, he'd thrown open the door and scrambled out, clutching his side. Then he was running at a staggering gait directly down the tarmac.

That turned out to be a fatal mistake. Moore simply slid in behind the wheel, gunned the engine and went racing after the injured man. Wentland was struck from behind, driven under the wheels of his own vehicle. Then, as he lay mortally wounded on the ground, Conner got out and attacked him, first pummeling him with his fists and then plunging the knife in over a dozen times.

Steven Wentland was dead, but that left Conner and Moore with a problem. What were they going to do with the body? Conner suggested that they drag Wentland into the brush by the roadside and then drive to his place of employment, a warehouse just a few miles away. There they could wash up and think things through.

But the terror of this dreadful night was not yet over. Indeed, it had only just begun. At the warehouse, Conner and Moore got into an argument about what to do with Wentland's body. Conner resolved it by fetching a sawed-off shotgun from his locker and shooting Moore to death. He then drove away, leaving the body where it lay. There was a witness to take care of. Bruce Voge was sprawled out on the couch at Tony Moore's house when Conner entered holding the shotgun. Voge never stood a chance.

Three young men were now dead, killed within the space of an hour over a petty argument. Conner, the sole survivor of the group, must have realized he was in deep trouble, but he still took the time to recruit some friends who would help him get rid of Moore's body. Then he hopped a Greyhound, heading out of town in the direction of Texas.

Conner's life on the run did not last long. Just four days later, he was picked up in Amarillo as he was about to board a bus for California. He was returned to Indiana to face murder charges with the prosecutor making it clear from the start that he intended seeking the death penalty.

Kevin Conner went on trial for three counts of capital murder in October 1988. Found guilty on all charges, he received death sentences for the murders of Moore and Voge, and a 60-year prison term for killing Steven Wentland. He showed little remorse nor emotion at the sentences. In fact, he said that he wanted no appeals lodged on his behalf. He wanted to die.

On July 27, 2005, Conner got his wish when he was put to death by lethal injection. Before his execution, he admitted to one more murder, that of fellow inmate Jerry Thompson, who'd died during an attempted prison break in 2002. Conner dined heartily on his last night on earth, consuming four chili dogs, a banana split and an Oreo-cookie Blizzard. He delivered an expletive-laced final statement, ending with the words: "Everybody has to die sometime, so let's get on with the killing."

Larry Gene Bell

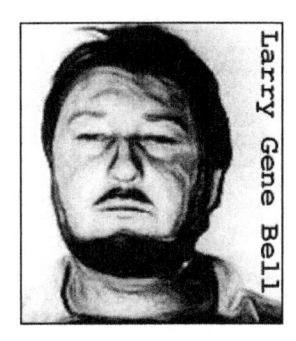

Larry Gene Bell was born on October 30, 1949, in Ralph, Alabama. His family appears to have lived a somewhat shiftless existence, moving frequently around the south. By the time he finished high school in 1967, Larry had lived in several states, including Alabama, Mississippi and South Carolina. It was Columbia, South Carolina, that he considered home, though, and after graduation, he returned there, started an apprenticeship as an electrician, and eventually married and fathered a son. He joined the Marines in 1970, but his military career lasted less than a year before he was discharged after accidentally shooting himself in the knee. Returning to his hometown, Bell worked for a short time as a prison guard before moving his family to Rock Hill, South Carolina. In 1976, he and his wife divorced.

So far there was very little in Larry Gene Bell's history to suggest the sadistic killer he would become. Serial killers often have extensive police records for lesser crimes before they cross the line into murder, but that was not the case with Bell. He was of no interest to the authorities until the day in 1984 when he abducted, raped and murdered Sandee Elaine Cornett in Charlotte, North Carolina. Cornett's body was never recovered, and although there was evidence linking Bell to the crime, it was not enough to make a case for murder. Investigators were forced to let the matter drop. This would have tragic consequences for two young girls.

At around 3:15 p.m. on Friday, May 31, 1985, 17-year-old Shari Faye Smith arrived at her parents' home in Lexington County, South Carolina. Shari's father saw her park her car at the end of the long driveway and get out, presumably to check the mailbox. When the car was still there minutes later, he became concerned and went to investigate. He found the vehicle's engine running but no sign of Shari. Bob Smith then carried out a frantic search of the area. Unable to find his daughter, he ran back to the house and called the police.

A search would eventually turn up Shari Smith's brutalized corpse on June 5. But the body might never have been found at all had the abductor not taunted the FBI with cryptic clues as to its location. At the same time, he'd also been harassing Shari's distraught parents with frequent phone calls. The Smiths also received a letter in Shari's handwriting, apparently drafted under instruction of her kidnapper. Entitled "Last Will and Testament," it read in part: "I'll be with my Father now. Please do not become hard or upset. Everything works out for the good for those that love the Lord."

Following the discovery of Shari's body, Bell continued to make his sickening phone calls to the Smith family. Over the next three weeks, he callously described how he'd abducted Shari at gunpoint, raped and sodomized her, then wrapped duct tape around her mouth and nose and watched her suffocate. In one call, he boasted about another murder and gave directions to the location of the victim's body. Following those instructions, the police were able to locate the remains of 10-year-old Debra May Helmick who'd gone missing from Richland County, South Carolina, two weeks after Shari Smith's abduction.

But Bell's taunting of the Smith family would eventually come back to haunt him. The paper on which Shari's "Last Will & Testament" had been written carried a faint impression of a telephone number which turned out to belong to Larry Gene Bell and led the police straight to his door. Evidence found inside his residence implicated him in the Smith and Helmick murders. Not that Bell was denying them anyway, he seemed almost keen to confess his crimes.

Larry Gene Bell was brought to trial in February 1986. He took the stand in his own defense and delivered six hours of bizarre testimony, during which he proclaimed himself to be Jesus Christ. Any question he did not want to answer was met with a petulant "Silence is golden." At one point during his testimony he even blurted out: "I want Dawn E. Smith to marry me!" Dawn was the sister of his victim, Shari.

But if this behavior was an attempt at an insanity defense, it failed. Bell was found guilty of murder and sentenced to die. He was put to death in South Carolina's electric chair on October 4, 1996, still proclaiming that he was the second coming of Christ.

Glen McGinnis

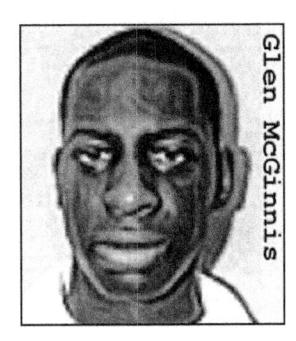

On the afternoon of August 1, 1990, a man named Homer Burson walked into Wilkins Dry Cleaners in Conroe, Texas, to pick up some cleaning. No one was in attendance, and so Burson waited a while at the counter before calling out for assistance. Getting no response, he left, only to return with another customer a few minutes later. It was then that he noticed the cash register was open. Burson then rounded the counter and walked towards the back of the store where he found the clerk, Leta Wilkerson, lying face up on the floor, covered in blood.

Burson staggered back from the gruesome sight and took a moment to compose himself before dialing 911. That brought police and an ambulance racing to the scene, but the latter arrived too late. Thirty-year-old Leta Wilkerson was dead. Three bullets to the back and one to the face had snuffed out her life.

A brutal murder had been committed, but the killer had been none too clever about it. There were .25-caliber casings scattered across the floor and a pile of jeans left on the counter, the name "McGinnis" written in the pockets. That turned out to be a valuable lead since a local youth named Glen McGinnis had been seen leaving the store shortly before Homer Burson had arrived there. McGinnis was well known to Conroe law officers, having acquired the first of his many arrests at the age of just 13. In fact, he'd only recently been bailed on misdemeanor assault and felony theft. And the motive here also appeared to be robbery. An estimated $140 had been taken from the register.

Also missing from the scene was Leta Wilkerson's 1985 silver-gray GMC minivan. An all-points bulletin was issued on the vehicle, and it delivered results that same evening when the van was found abandoned at a shopping mall. It was immediately dusted for prints and produced a match to the man who was by now the main suspect – Glen McGinnis. And there was an even more obvious clue. Lying between the two front seats, detectives found McGinnis's wallet. When employees at the mall picked McGinnis out of a photo array as the man who'd left the van there, an arrest warrant was issued.

Glen McGinnis was taken into custody at the Williams Square Apartments the following morning with detectives noting that his residence was just two blocks from the crime scene. In his possession, officers found $105 in cash for which he could provide no explanation. And then there was the .25-caliber Raven semi-automatic pistol, which officers found hidden in the laundry hamper. With that, McGinnis was arrested and charged with capital murder.

The case against McGinnis was overwhelming. There were eyewitnesses who'd seen him at the crime scene and witnesses who'd seen him in the victim's van; there was his wallet found inside the vehicle; there were fingerprints; there was the unexplained cash; and there was the 25-caliber pistol, now confirmed by ballistics to be the murder weapon. Aside from a witness who'd seen the actual shooting, the case was a prosecutor's dream.

And yet, McGinnis chose to plead not guilty at trial, when the wiser course might have been to admit culpability and beg the prosecutor for a deal. He was only 17, after all. That might have counted in his favor. Instead, McGinnis was found guilty and, in keeping with state law, he was condemned to death.

As always when the offender is a juvenile, there was outrage over the sentence. There were also several petitions for clemency. But Texas governors seldom grant concessions in capital cases, and current incumbent George W. Bush had issued only one pardon during his entire term in office. He was not about to start with a killer who'd gunned down an innocent woman and left two small children orphaned.

Glen McGinnis was put to death by lethal injection on January 25, 2000.

Buddy Earl Justus

Buddy Earl Justus was born in Niagara Falls, New York, on Christmas Day 1952. Soon after, his family moved to Roanoke, Virginia, where Buddy ended up being placed in an orphanage. By his late teens, he already had a lengthy police record, mainly for breaking and entering. One of those crimes would land him in the Montgomery County Jail. It was here that Buddy's life took a turn for the better.

Charlie Harris was a pastor who counseled inmates on matters of spirituality. Most simply ignored his guidance, but not Buddy Justus. He decided that he was going to turn his life around. Shortly after his release from prison, he married a woman named Alice, although the union was short-lived. Thereafter, Buddy returned to his hometown of Niagara Falls where he found work changing truck tires for the Tire Shoppe on Military Road. Buddy was a model employee, respectful, soft-spoken and reliable, even if he politely declined to work on weekends.

The reason for that refusal was never explained, and his employers didn't push the issue since Buddy was such a good worker. What they didn't know was that Buddy Justus, the polite southern gent and all-round good guy, moonlighted as a serial rapist on weekends, trawling the streets in his maroon-and-silver Chrysler Cordoba, looking for victims. And like many malefactors who follow that path, he'd soon graduate from serial rapist to serial killer.

On October 3, 1978, Justus broke into the double-wide trailer of Ida Mae Moses in Williamsburg, Virginia. The 21-year-old nurse was eight-and-a-half months pregnant, due to give birth in two weeks, and eagerly awaiting the arrival of her first child. But that didn't stop Justus robbing her, raping her, and shooting her three times in the head, killing both her and the unborn baby.

Justus then headed south, picking up 18-year-old hitchhiker Dale Dean Goins on his path. In Goins, Justus found a man of similarly warped personality. Shortly after hooking up, the pair kidnapped Rosemary Jackson, a 32-year-old housewife, as she left a grocery store in suburban Atlanta, Georgia. Rosemary was then driven to a remote area where she was raped by both of the men before being shot to death, her body dumped on a rural service road. Justus and Goins headed next to Florida where they snatched 21-year-old Stephanie Michelle Hawkins from a shopping mall. Stephanie was raped and killed in a near duplicate of the Jackson murder.

But by now, police in Virginia were onto Justus. His distinctive car had been seen parked outside Ida Mae Moses' trailer on the day she was killed. Buddy's employers at the Tire Shoppe, still wondering what might have happened to their ultra-reliable employee, were astonished when detectives arrived to question them about his whereabouts. Meanwhile, officers were also staking out the orphanage in Grundy, Virginia, where Justus had been raised and where two of his siblings still lived. Buddy Justus was arrested when he came to visit on October 11, 1978.

Under interrogation, Justus admitted that he had robbed and murdered Ida Mae Moses. However, despite strong evidence to the contrary, he denied raping her. That denial did him no good at all. Found guilty at trial, he was sentenced to die in the electric chair.

Subsequent death penalties would follow in Florida and in Georgia, but it was the state of Virginia that would put Justus to death. At exactly 11 p.m. on December 13, 1990, Buddy Earl Justus was strapped into the electric chair at the Virginia State Penitentiary in Richmond. Six minutes and two jolts of electricity later, he was pronounced dead.

Justus' accomplice, Dale Dean Goins, was sentenced to life in prison in Florida for the murder of Stephanie Michelle Hawkins.

William Hickman

On December 15, 1927, a well-dressed young man showed up at Mount Vernon Junior High School in Los Angeles. He said that he was there to collect 12-year-old Marion Parker on behalf of her father, Perry Parker. Asked for his credentials, the man suggested that they phone Mr. Parker at the bank that he managed. School officials didn't do that, though. Instead, they released Marion into the man's care. What they didn't realize was that they'd just delivered the little girl into the hands of a kidnapper.

Marion's disappearance only came to light when Parker got home that evening and found that his daughter wasn't there. Then Marion's twin, Marjorie, told him that a man had picked Marion up from school, apparently on his instructions. Parker had just about processed that startling piece of information when a special delivery letter arrived, informing him that his daughter had been kidnapped and demanding a ransom of $1,500. It also warned him not to contact the authorities. Parker, nonetheless, phoned the police immediately.

LAPD Chief of Detectives Herman Cline took personal charge of the investigation. His first action was to question staff at the Mount Vernon School. Based on their input, an all-points bulletin was issued for a young, dark-haired man, driving a Ford Roadster and accompanied by a girl matching Marion's description.

The following day, December 16, a letter arrived, telling Parker to be ready with the ransom money and to wait by the phone. At around 8 p.m., the kidnapper called, provided a location for the drop, and instructed Parker to come alone. Parker did as he was told, but the kidnapper failed to show. The following day another letter arrived in which the kidnapper chastised Parker for disobeying his instruction by having the police tail him. He then offered Parker one last chance to get his daughter back alive with a new drop set for that evening.

This time Parker insisted that the police stand down. At 7:45, he was parked at the designated spot when a black coupe pulled up beside him. The man at the wheel wore a white bandanna over his mouth and nose. Parker could see his daughter sitting in the passenger seat, a blanket wrapped around her. He handed over the money when the kidnapper demanded it and waited while he counted it. When the man said that he was going to drive to the end of the block and drop Marion there, Parker agreed. He then watched the black coupe drive the short distance and stop momentarily to drop a bundle into the street before racing off.

The kidnapper had barely fled the scene when Parker was racing towards the bundle. It was Marion alright, but she was dead and horribly mutilated. Both of her legs had been cut off. So too had her arms below the elbow. Her eyes were wide open, the eyelids sewn to the forehead with black thread. An autopsy would later determine that she'd also been eviscerated, the organs removed and the body cavity stuffed with rags.

The kidnapping of Marion Parker had now become the savage murder of an innocent 12-year-old, and the police responded accordingly. A massive manhunt was launched, involving thousands of officers. On Sunday, December 18, a man was walking his dog in an L.A. park when he discovered Marion's severed legs and forearms. A day later, the police found the suspect's Ford Roadster and were able to lift a single fingerprint. It belonged to 19-year-old William Edward Hickman, a petty thief and sometime forger. Hickman matched the description of the man who'd taken Marion. Before long, his mugshot was gracing the front page of every newspaper across the country.

Hickman was captured in Oregon on December 22 when he was pulled over while driving a stolen car. Extradited to California, he admitted kidnapping but blamed Marion's murder on an accomplice. Unfortunately for Hickman, the man he named had the perfect alibi. He was in prison at the time of the abduction and murder. Faced with the mounting evidence against him, Hickman finally broke down and confessed.

Hickman's trial began in Los Angeles in January 1928, with his defense lodging an insanity plea. Their strategy, however, would be blown out of the water when Hickman was caught passing a note to a prison buddy. "You know, and I know, that I am not insane," it read. Once the note was read out in court, Hickman's fate was sealed. It took the jury just 36 minutes to find him guilty of first-degree murder. The offense carried a mandatory sentence of death by hanging.

William Hickman went to the gallows at San Quentin on October 19, 1928. The execution, however, was badly botched. The drop was miscalculated and rather than suffering the swift neck break that hanging usually delivers, Hickman was throttled to death, taking ten minutes to die.

Steve Roach

Steve Roach had endured a tumultuous childhood, with parents who were often at each other's throats and separated four times while he was growing up, only to later get back together again. Part of the problem was Roach's father's many health problems, making him reliant on medication that caused extreme mood swings. He was also a heavy drinker and a womanizer who sometimes brought his conquests home. Roach's parents also paid scant attention to their son's education, pulling him out of school at 14 because they needed him to look after his younger brothers.

Despite all of these difficulties, Steve Roach grew to be a respectful and well-mannered boy. He was a regular churchgoer and a volunteer at children's summer camps; he could be relied upon to do odd jobs for friends and neighbors; he was a great help to the elderly in his neighborhood. Mamie Estes and her sister Mary Ann Hughes, in particular, had reason to thank Steve. He chopped their wood and cut their lawn. On occasion, he'd even join the old ladies for a few hands of Yahtzee. Which makes it all the more difficult to understand why he ended up shot-gunning one of them to death

It happened on December 3, 1993. On that day, Mary Ann Hughes was found lying dead in the doorway of her home outside of Stanardsville, Virginia. The 70-year-old had been shot at close range with a shotgun, the pellets ripping through her face and pulping her brain. A search of the scene indicated that the victim's purse had been taken, along with her black Buick Regal. The police also learned that 17-year-old Steve Roach, who was acquainted with the victim, had been seen firing a shotgun on his parents' property just a few days earlier. When they went to question him, they found that Roach was missing.

A statewide alert was issued for the missing teen and the stolen vehicle. However, Roach had already crossed the border into North Carolina. Over the next two days, he would remain at large, traversing the Carolinas, living off Mrs. Hughes' credit cards. At one location, he was caught on videotape making a withdrawal from an ATM.

On December 5, two days after the murder, a South Carolina Highway Patrol officer pulled Roach over for speeding. However, the fugitive was not about to be taken. He evaded arrest by fleeing on foot into the nearby woods. Later that evening, he called his aunt and was persuaded to turn himself in. A day later, he returned to Virginia and surrendered to Greene County Sheriff William Morris.

The crime committed by Steve Roach was a particularly heinous one. However, he made a pretty pathetic murder suspect. "I didn't mean to kill her," he whimpered at his trial. "The gun was only to scare her so that I could rob her."

Be that as it may, Steve Roach had gunned down a helpless, elderly woman who he had once declared was "like a grandmother" to him. It also turned out that Roach was not the paragon of virtue his defense sought to portray. In the year leading up to the murder, Roach had been arrested three times, twice for burglary and once for auto theft. That, according to the prosecutor, made him a menace to society. And the jury agreed. They found Roach guilty of murder and recommended that he should pay the ultimate price.

Steve Roach was put to death by lethal injection on January 13, 2000. He was 23 years old on the day that he died, 17 years old on the day he committed the crime that sent him to death row. "I am not afraid to die," he said in his final statement. "I know that I'll wake up in heaven."

Charles Brooks Jr.

The method by which judicial executions have been carried out has gone through many iterations down the centuries, from such barbaric practices as breaking on the wheel and drawing and quartering, to more "humane" methods like electrocution, gassing, and hanging. The modern method of choice (at least in the United States) is a form of euthanasia delivered via a cocktail of lethal drugs (or sometimes by a single drug). This method has been in effect since 1982, and the first U.S. inmate to be put to death in this way was a man named Charles Brooks Jr.

In many ways, Charles Brooks makes an unlikely death row inmate. Raised in a middle-class Fort Worth family, he had done well in school and been a regular starter on the football team. After graduation, he dabbled with drugs but was by no means a hardcore user. He was also not a hardened criminal, although he did serve a term at Leavenworth for illegal possession of firearms. In fact, the worst thing that could be said about Charles Brooks was that he should have been more particular about the company he kept.

One of the lowlifes that Brooks regularly hung out with was a man named Woody Lourdes. Lourdes had a girlfriend, a heroin-addicted prostitute named Marlene Smith, who was also an enthusiastic shoplifter. On the morning of December 14, 1976, Smith traded sexual services with a local car dealer for the use of a car for the day. She then drove to a liquor store on Rosedale Avenue where she knew Lourdes and Brooks would be hanging out. There, she encouraged the men to join her on a "shopping trip" (a shoplifting expedition) to the south side of Fort Worth.

But Smith had been short changed in her 'sex for transport' deal. The car she'd been given was a clunker, and within a few miles, it had broken down. Brooks and Lourdes were forced to push it to a nearby gas station where all attempts to get it started failed.

The trio were now stranded. But then Brooks had an idea. He told the other two to wait at the car while he walked to a nearby lot to "get a car to test drive." This he did, although there was a small wrinkle he hadn't anticipated. The company insisted that one of their employees accompany him on the drive. The man chosen for the job was a young mechanic named David Gregory.

Behind the wheel of the test vehicle, Brooks now had a problem. How was he going to get rid of his escort? Forcing him from the vehicle at gunpoint was obviously an option, but Gregory would then raise the alarm and every cop in the area would be looking out for the stolen car. No, Brooks decided, they were going to have to take Gregory along with them. By the time he pulled to a stop beside their broken-down ride, he knew what to do. Drawing his gun, he forced Gregory from the car and then into the trunk. He and Lourdes then got into the vehicle and drove away. Smith, having witnessed the gunpoint abduction, remained behind, saying she wanted nothing to do with it.

The events of the next few hours have been the subject of much conjecture, both at the trial and in its aftermath. We know that Lourdes and Brooks drove into the parking lot at the New Lincoln Motel at about 6:00 p.m., forced Gregory from the trunk and frog-marched him to Room 17 where Lourdes was staying at the time. A short while later, shots were heard, and the motel manager called the police. They arrived to find David Gregory bound to a chair with coat hangers and shot in the head. Of Lourdes and Brooks, there was no sign. They had been seen driving away from the motel a short time before the police got there. They were arrested later that night at the house of a friend.

Now began a protracted quest for justice, complicated by the fact that neither of the accused would say who had fired the fatal shot. Both would ultimately be convicted of first-degree murder, although their sentences were markedly different. Lourdes got 40 years in prison. Charles Brooks was sentenced to death.

At just after midnight on December 7, 1982, Charles Brooks entered the history books as the first inmate to be executed by lethal injection in the United States. The execution went off without a hitch and was heralded a complete success.

Donald 'Pee Wee' Gaskins

Born in South Carolina on March 31, 1933, Donald Henry Gaskins grew up to be a runt of a boy who attracted the nickname "Pee Wee" due to his diminutive build. But looks were deceiving in Pee Wee's case. From his early years, he was a problem child, a thief and a bully, with a precocious interest in sex, who was in and out of state reformatories throughout his youth. Dropping out of school at the age of just 14, he joined up with two other juvenile delinquents and ranged around the area committing burglaries and rapes. Their spree was eventually ended when Gaskins was arrested for clubbing a teenaged victim with a hatchet during a burglary. That saw him sent back to the reformatory where he remained until 1951.

Released on his 18th birthday, Gaskins made a token effort to go straight. But he was soon back inside after he was convicted of attacking a woman with a hammer. It was while serving this sentence that Gaskins committed his first known murder, slitting the throat of a fellow inmate who had tried to rape him. Convicted of manslaughter, Pee Wee had nine years added to his sentence. But he had no intention of serving that time. In 1955, he pulled off a daring prison break and fled to Tennessee. Recaptured soon after, he drew an additional three years, eventually gaining parole in August 1961. He'd barely walked free when he was in trouble again, arrested for the statutory rape of a 12-year-old girl. That brought yet another prison term, keeping him behind bars until November 1968.

By now, Gaskins had built up a seething hatred towards society in general and women in particular. His only release came through violence, and so he took to cruising the Carolina coastline looking for hitchhikers to rape and kill. The first of these so-called "Coastal Kills" was committed in September 1969 when he picked up a random woman, tortured and disemboweled her, and then dumped her mutilated remains in the ocean. Within a year, he had committed ten similarly horrific murders.

Coastal Kills, by Gaskins' definition, were purely for gratification. Where he killed for gain, or to conceal evidence of another crime, he used a different label. He called these "Serious Murders."

The first of Gaskins' Serious Murders was committed in November 1969 when he raped and killed his own niece, 15-year-old Janice Kirby, and her friend, 17-year-old Patricia Alsbrook. Gaskins had asked the girls to have sex with him. When they refused he strangled and beat them, then drowned them in a barrel and buried their bodies in shallow graves.

Over the years that followed, Gaskins' murder spree went on unabated. He continued to cruise the coastal roads looking for victims while also dispatching criminal accomplices and personal enemies. At the same time, he preyed on female acquaintances, raping and killing those who aroused him sexually. One of the worst cases, involved the rape-slayings of 23-year-old Doreen Dempsey and her 20-month-old daughter, Robin. Dempsey had made the mistake of accepting a ride from Gaskins, who she regarded as a friend. Gaskins would later describe raping the infant as the best sexual experience of his life.

By 1975, Pee Wee Gaskins was 42 years of age and had been killing steadily for over six years. The main reason he'd managed to evade detection was because he worked alone, never involving anyone else in his murders. But that was to change after he committed a triple homicide and needed help in getting rid of the bodies. The man he enlisted was an ex-con named Walter Neely, and Neely then became a regular accomplice. Unfortunately for Gaskins, Neely wasn't the sharpest tool in the shed. After being arrested for auto theft, he started talking and had soon led investigators to the shallow graves of eight murder victims.

Gaskins was arrested, charged, convicted and ultimately sentenced to death. He then tried bargaining for his life, giving up details of his many other crimes in the hope of having his sentence commuted. That turned out to be a bad move. In 1976, the U.S. Supreme Court placed a moratorium on capital punishment, and Gaskins' sentence was commuted anyway. By the time it was reinstated in 1978, Gaskins had been convicted of eight more murders and was serving nine life terms with no possibility of parole.

Pee Wee Gaskins might well have seen out the rest of his days behind bars, but with a man like Pee Wee, that was never likely to happen. In 1982, he accepted a contract to kill death-row inmate Randolph Tyner, a contract he fulfilled by packing a transistor radio with explosives and detonating it while Tyner held it to his ear.

This time there would be no respite for Gaskins. Found guilty of murder, he was sentenced to death and executed in the electric chair on September 6, 1991. He left behind a handwritten "autobiography" in which he claimed responsibility for over 100 murders.

Toronto Patterson

Toronto Patterson was a 17-year-old street punk, a wannabe tough guy who'd been dealing drugs since the age of 15. Extremely defiant of authority, he openly wore his gang colors to school and carried a beeper which he'd respond to even if it went off in the middle of class. When the school authorities tried to take the beeper away from him, he threatened to kill them. And he wasn't kidding. That same year, he'd fired a Mac-12 machine pistol at an acquaintance. He'd also been arrested for being in possession of a 9 mm handgun.

Eventually, in 1994, Patterson stopped attending school altogether and started dealing drugs full time. Why wouldn't he? He was a teenaged delinquent, earning 500 to 700 dollars a day, driving a BMW and decking himself out in gold jewelry. He felt like he had it made.

But even this wasn't enough. Like most criminals, Patterson remained covetous of the possessions of others, and the one thing he particularly wanted were the expensive gold mag wheels off his cousin's BMW. Vernon Stiff was currently serving time at the State Penitentiary and storing the vehicle at the home of Evelyn Stiff, Patterson's aunt. On June 6, 1995, Patterson decided to take what he wanted.

At around 10 a.m. on that day, Patterson left his girlfriend's house and drove to the Stiff residence. Evelyn wasn't at home, but Patterson's cousin, Kimberly Brewer was, along with her daughters, six-year-old Jennifer and three-year-old Ollie. This was a potential obstacle to his plan, but Patterson played it cool. He sat chatting with Kimberley for about 15 minutes, then left, saying that he had to attend a physical therapy session.

Kimberley didn't expect to see her cousin again that day, but about an hour later, he was back, walking up the drive in his exaggerated gangster strut. Then, as he entered the house, he drew a .38-revolver and fired, hitting Kimberley in the head and killing her instantly. He then walked to the children's bedroom where he found Ollie and Jennifer watching cartoons. Sparing no thought for familial loyalties, or for the tender ages of his victims, he opened fire. Jennifer was shot in the head as she cowered on the floor. Ollie was killed as she lay on the bed with her hands covering her ears in a piteous attempt at self-preservation. Three bullets passed through her left hand and into her neck and skull.

Having so brutally slain three members of his family, Patterson walked calmly to the garage where he removed three wheels from the BMW. Unable to remove the fourth, he was forced to leave it behind. Later that afternoon, he tried to sell the wheels to the owner of a tire shop but was refused because the set was incomplete. He then drove to his girlfriend's house and stashed the wheels in her garage for safe-keeping.

But already the police were onto Patterson. Valarie Brewer, who had discovered the bodies of her sister and nieces, informed the police that Patterson had recently had the wheels stolen off his car and might therefore have wanted the ones from his cousin's vehicle. He was tracked down and arrested that same day, still wearing the blood-spattered tracksuit he'd worn while committing the triple homicide. When police carried out a search at his girlfriend's house and found the stolen wheels, the game was all but up for him.

Patterson, though, wasn't about to accept responsibility. First, he tried to pin the killings on "two Jamaicans." Then, after police revealed that they had found the stolen wheels at his girlfriend's house, he broke down and confessed. Later, he'd withdraw that confession, claiming that the police had coerced it from him.

Patterson would eventually stand trial for only one murder, that of three-year-old Ollie Brewer. The prosecutor's intent in this was clear. The murder of a person under the age of six years is automatically a capital offense in the state of Texas. Once the jury found Patterson guilty, there could be only one outcome.

Toronto Patterson was put to death by lethal injection on August 28, 2002, maintaining his innocence to the end. "I am sorry for the pain, sorry for what I caused my friends, family, and loved ones," he said in his last statement. "But I do not think I should die for a crime I did not commit."

Christopher Emmett

John Langley and Christopher Emmett weren't buddies exactly, but they got along well enough to room together when they were doing out-of-town work. The two men were employed as roofers by Weldon Roofing Company, operating out of Roanoke Rapids, North Carolina. During April of 2001, they'd been dispatched to a worksite in Danville, Virginia. It was there that the trouble started.

The evening of April 26, 2001, had started pleasantly enough. The workers had retired to their motel, tired after a hard day's work. Langley had bought groceries and had grilled some food for his colleagues. They'd drunk beer and played cards. Then Emmett and another member of the crew, Michael Pittman, had approached Langley for a loan, saying they wanted to buy some crack cocaine. Langley had given them the money, and they'd left the motel soon after. The other workers had stayed up for a while longer and then retired to bed.

At around 11:00 p.m., Rainey Bell, another member of the work crew, heard a loud banging sound coming from the room that Emmett and Langley were sharing. About an hour later, just after midnight, a somewhat disheveled Emmett stumbled into the motel's reception and asked the desk clerk to call the police. He said that he'd just returned to his room and had seen "blood and stuff."

Officers arrived at the motel at around 12:45 a.m. and accompanied Emmett back to his room where they found John Langley lying face down on a bed. Blood spatters on the sheets, on the headboard, on the wall behind it spoke of a savage attack, with the most likely weapon a heavy brass lamp, lying damaged on the floor. The obvious suspect was Christopher Emmett, but he denied killing his roommate. According to him, he'd gone out and had returned to find Langley already dead.

The evidence, however, contradicted Emmett's version of events. Blood spatters on his hands, on his boots, on his clothing, could only have gotten there if he'd been present while Langley was being clubbed with the lamp. Emmett was therefore taken to the station for questioning. There, he continued to deny involvement in Langley's death, offering several versions of what had happened. Caught in one lie too many, he eventually cracked and admitted clubbing Langley to death.

According to Emmett's confession, he and Langley had gotten into an altercation after Langley refused to loan him more money to buy additional cocaine. During that confrontation, he'd picked up the lamp and struck Langley "five or six times" rendering him unconscious. He'd then taken Langley's wallet, and he and Pittman had left the motel to buy more cocaine. It was when he returned that he'd realized Langley was dead.

It was a senseless killing, committed on the spur of the moment by a man strung out on crack cocaine. However, it had also been committed during the commission of another felony, the theft of John Langley's wallet. That made it an aggravated homicide and thus liable for the death penalty under the laws of the Commonwealth of Virginia. There was also evidence presented at trial that this was not the first death caused by Christopher Emmett. Emmett had killed before, knocking over a motorcyclist while driving under the influence. Apparently, on that occasion, he'd jokingly told medical staff not to bother trying to assist the fatally injured man. "I already checked," he'd smirked. "He's done."

Emmett was similarly flippant about the murder of John Langley. Asked why he'd bludgeoned his co-worker to death, he smiled and said that it had "seemed like the right thing to do at the time." That callous attitude would come back to haunt him when the jury found him guilty of capital murder and recommended the death penalty, a sanction later ratified by the trial judge.

Christopher Scott Emmett was put to death by lethal injection on July 24, 2008. His last words were typical of the man. "Tell my family and friends I love them. Tell the governor he just lost my vote. Y'all hurry this along, I'm dying to get out of here."

Earle Nelson

Born in Philadelphia on May 12, 1897, Earle Nelson was orphaned at the age of just fifteen months when his father died of syphilis, a disease that had also claimed his mother six months earlier. He was then shipped off to San Francisco into the care of his staunchly religious grandmother. Adopting some of her fanaticism, he became obsessed with the Bible, even if his behavior did not match its tenets. From a young age, he was a persistent shoplifter, and also a bully who was expelled from school due to his violent temper.

At age eleven, Earle suffered a serious head injury when he was struck by a streetcar while riding his bicycle. Three years later, there was an even more traumatic event – his grandmother died, leaving him devastated. Shortly thereafter, Earle was sent to live with his Aunt Lillian and dropped out of school. Just 14 years old, he began work as a manual laborer, although he seldom held a job for very long. By 15, he was drinking heavily and visiting prostitutes; at 18, he served his first prison term for burglary.

Emerging from prison two years later, Nelson enlisted in the Army, although his outlandish behavior would soon land him in the Napa State Mental Hospital. He'd spend 18 months at Napa, escaping three times before the Army eventually tired of his behavior and discharged him. He then returned to San Francisco and found work as a janitor at St. Mary's Hospital. There, the 21-year-old Earle fell in love with a 58-year-old co-worker, Mary Martin. Eventually he persuaded Mary to marry him, but Mary would soon regret saying yes. Earle's bizarre habits and insatiable sex drive drove her to a nervous breakdown.

In 1921, Nelson suffered a second serious head injury when he fell from a ladder at work. Thereafter, he complained of hearing voices and became increasingly violent and paranoid. On May 19, 1921, he dragged a 12-year-old girl into a basement and tried to strangle her, fleeing the scene when she started screaming. Captured soon after, he was returned to Napa State Hospital where he would remain until 1925. Thereafter, he hit the road. Earle Nelson was about to make the transition from petty criminal to serial murderer.

The first woman to fall victim to the "Dark Strangler" was Clara Newmann, a 62-year-old widow who ran a boarding house in San Francisco. Newmann was strangled to death and posthumously raped after she allowed Nelson to view a room for rent. A little over two weeks later, another landlady, Laura Beal, died in almost identical circumstances. Then, on June 16, 1926, Lillian St. Mary was strangled, throwing the city into a panic. Nelson then made his way south to Santa Barbara where he strangled Mrs. Olivia Russell. He followed that up with killings in Oakland and in Portland, Oregon. By the end of 1926, he'd already murdered fourteen women and had also suffocated an eight-month-old baby.

With the Northwest in a state of virtual siege, Nelson headed east, stopping in Iowa, Kansas City, and Philadelphia. He then made his way to Buffalo, New York, Detroit and Chicago before turning west again. He'd already killed 20 women in the United States by the time be showed up in Winnipeg, Canada.

Shortly after Nelson's arrival in the town, 14-year-old Lola Cowan went missing while selling paper flowers door to door on the street where Nelson was living. Lola had not yet been found when a man named William Patterson came home from work and discovered his wife, Emily, raped and strangled to death. The police then carried out a search of all residences in the area and found Lola Cowan's decomposing corpse hidden under the bed in Nelson's room.

But Nelson had already fled town and was making his way back to the border. And he may well have made it had an alert storeowner in Wakopa not recognized him and alerted the authorities. When the local constable arrived with his revolver drawn, Nelson surrendered without a fight.

Within weeks of his capture, Earle Nelson was charged with murders in San Francisco, Portland, Detroit, Philadelphia, and Buffalo. It was clear, however, that he'd never see the inside of an American courtroom. The Canadian authorities were determined to punish him for the crimes he'd committed in their jurisdiction.

Earle Nelson went on trial for the murders of Lola Cowan and Emily Patterson in November 1927. Despite his proclamations of innocence, there was never any doubt as to the outcome. Found guilty, he was sentenced to hang. He went to the gallows on January 13, 1928, maintaining to the end that he was innocent.

John Rook

It was an audacious kidnapping committed in broad daylight on a city street in Raleigh, North Carolina. The victim was Ann Marie Roche, a pretty young nurse with long blonde hair worn in a ponytail. Her abductor, a white male of somewhat disheveled appearance, had dragged his victim into a car and then sped off with her. The date was May 12, 1980.

How on earth the abductor thought he would get away with this was never documented for the record. He was hardly likely to escape detection. The vehicle he'd spirited his victim away in was easily traced since an eyewitness had written down the license plate number. Its owner, a man living in the Raleigh suburbs, was astonished when armed police stormed his property later that same day. Under questioning, he confirmed that the car was his but insisted that he hadn't driven it that day. He'd loaned it to a neighbor named John Rook. In fact, Rook was late in returning the car, and he was none too happy about it.

With the vehicle owner's alibi confirmed, the police switched gears and put out a bulletin on 21-year-old John Rook, warning that he might be armed and dangerous. The fugitive was eventually captured three days later on May 15. By then, Ann Marie Roche's brutalized corpse had already been found in a field several miles outside the city limits. The once vivacious young woman had been savagely raped, brutally beaten, and then killed in the most heinous way possible. Her attacker had driven his car over her as she lay injured on the ground.

John Rook was no stranger to law enforcement. He had an extensive record which included arrests for indecently assaulting a minor and for DUI. He also had numerous arrests for assaults on women and had served time for beating up a former girlfriend. Under interrogation, he told officers that he had a drinking problem and did stupid things while he was "under the influence." However, he wouldn't confess to abducting, raping and killing Ann Marie Roche until one of the interrogators suggested to him that it took a strong man to admit that he'd made a mistake. Then Rook suddenly blurted out. "Okay, I did it. I hope you're happy." He then provided additional details about the crime, leaving the police in no doubt that they had the right man.

Rook was charged with rape, kidnapping, and first-degree murder. By the time the matter came to trial in October 1980, he'd had a change of heart, withdrawing his confession and pleading not guilty on all charges. But the confession wasn't needed in this case. The evidence against Rook was exceptionally strong and included eyewitness testimony, forensics (including tire tracks and fiber evidence) and the incriminating statements he'd made to detectives while under Miranda. Nobody was surprised when he was found guilty of first-degree murder and sentenced to death.

John Rook would not go easily to his death. He filed appeals based on the admissibility of statements made to the police and on his state of inebriation at the time of the murder. All of these were rejected. So too was his clemency appeal. He was put to death by lethal injection on September 19, 1986.

Kenneth Biros

On the evening of February 7, 1991, Tami Engstrom left her job at the Clover Bar in Hubbard, Ohio, claiming that she was feeling unwell. Tami's mother Pat, who also worked at the Clover, advised her to go home and get straight into bed, but Tami ignored that advice. Instead, she drove to the Nickelodeon Lounge in Masury, Ohio, a regular watering hole of her favorite uncle. Tami arrived at Nickelodeon at around 10:00 and remained until 1:00 a.m. by which time she'd had quite a lot to drink and was barely able to stand.

Also in the bar that night was a man named Kenneth Biros. Solidly built with medium length auburn hair and a reddish mustache, Biros was a regular at the Nickelodeon and knew most of the locals, including Tami's uncle. He did not know Tami, but he appeared fixated on the pretty, vivacious blonde. When it appeared that Tami was not going to be able to drive herself home, Biros suggested a local diner where she could have a few cups of strong coffee to sober up. Tami drove away from the

Nickelodeon's parking lot with Ken Biros at around 1:15 a.m. No one, bar her killer, would ever see her alive again.

While all of this was going on, Tami's husband, Andy, had been frantically searching for her. Andy had finished his late shift at 11 and had driven to the Clover Bar, only to find that his wife had already left. He'd then driven home, expecting her to be there. She wasn't. Neither was she with any of her family, although her sister Debi suggested that she might have gone to the Nickelodeon. Andy then called the bar and learned that Tami had been there but had just left with her uncle. Content now that his wife was safe and would soon be home, Andy went to bed. By the time he woke the next morning, Tami had still not returned. It was then that he phoned Tami's uncle and learned that she'd left the bar with Kenneth Biros.

Sick with anger and worry, Andy drove to Biros' home and confronted the man. Biros seemed surprised by the outburst. He admitted that he'd left the Nickelodeon with Tami but said that she'd jumped from his car on the way to the diner and run away. He'd assumed that she'd made it back to her vehicle and had driven home.

Biros would repeat that story several times over the next two days, including to the police in Sharon, Pennsylvania, after they became involved in the search. On the afternoon of Saturday, February 9, he was asked to come down to the station to answer some questions. Captain John Klaric conducted the interview and immediately noticed fresh scratches on Biros' hands and a cut over his right eye. Asked about these injuries, Biros said that he'd cut himself while smashing a window to get into his house. Klaric let it slide and asked Biros to talk him through his last encounter with Tami Engstrom. This Biros did, sticking to the same storyline.

However, as Klaric continued to probe, Biros suddenly blurted out that he had done something "very bad." Klaric then asked him to explain, and Biros offered a different version of his story. He now claimed that they'd been driving along some railroad tracks when he'd reached over and put his hand on Tami's leg. That had "freaked her out" and she'd thrown open the door and jumped from the moving vehicle, striking her head against the rail tracks in the process. Biros had then panicked. Certain that he'd be blamed for her death, he'd decided to bury the body.

On Sunday, February 10, 1991, Biros led officers to Tami Engstrom's body, buried in a remote wooded area of Butler County, Pennsylvania. The condition of the remains, however, did not fit with the story he'd told. Tami had been sickeningly mutilated. Her head and right breast had been hacked from the body; her right leg had been amputated just above the knee; her torso had been cut open and most of the organs had been removed; the anus and vagina had been cut from the corpse and were missing. Clearly a lot more had happened than what Biros was admitting.

Biros, however, wasn't accepting responsibility. By the time the matter came to court, he'd changed his story again, now claiming the Tami had attacked him and that he'd killed her in self-defense. He'd only cut her up, he said, because the hole he'd dug to bury the body was too small. It was a quite ludicrous story, especially as the autopsy proved that the cause of death was strangulation.

Kenneth Biros was found guilty of murder and sentenced to death. His execution, carried out on December 8, 2009, was a landmark one. It was the first time a U.S. inmate was put to death by a single drug rather than the three-drug cocktail typically used in judicial executions.

For more True Crime books by Robert Keller please visit

http://bit.ly/kellerbooks

Printed in Great Britain
by Amazon